A MATTER OF TIME

Positioning your children to change their world one moment at a time

GALEN WOODWARD

Foreword by Dustin Woodward

WESTBOW
PRESS®
A DIVISION OF THOMAS NELSON
& ZONDERVAN

This book is a work of non-fiction. Unless otherwise noted, the author and the publisher make no explicit guarantees as to the accuracy of the information contained in this book and in some cases, names of people and places have been altered to protect their privacy.

WestBow Press books may be ordered through booksellers or by contacting:

WestBow Press
A Division of Thomas Nelson & Zondervan
1663 Liberty Drive
Bloomington, IN 47403
www.westbowpress.com
844-714-3454

Because of the dynamic nature of the Internet, any web addresses or links contained in this book may have changed since publication and may no longer be valid. The views expressed in this work are solely those of the author and do not necessarily reflect the views of the publisher, and the publisher hereby disclaims any responsibility for them.

Any people depicted in stock imagery provided by Getty Images are models, and such images are being used for illustrative purposes only. Certain stock imagery © Getty Images.

All Scripture quotations are taken from The Holy Bible, New International Version®, NIV® Copyright © 1973, 1978, 1984, 2011 by Biblica, Inc.® Used by permission. All rights reserved worldwide.

ISBN: 978-1-6642-0219-1 (sc)
ISBN: 978-1-6642-0218-4 (hc)
ISBN: 978-1-6642-0220-7 (e)

Library of Congress Control Number: 2020915662

Print information available on the last page.

WestBow Press rev. date: 12/10/2020

DEDICATION

This book is written in honor of my mom. Mom, it's impossible to thank you adequately for everything you've done, from loving me unconditionally to raising me in a stable, consistent household. You instilled Christian values in our family, teaching us to embrace and enjoy life. I could not have asked for a better mother.

When you need real understanding,
when you need someone to care,
when you need someone to listen,
a mother is always there.

CONTENTS

SECTION 3　FIVE CHARACTERISTICS OF A GENERATIONAL LEADER

SECTION 4　TIME TO BUILD YOUR LEGACY

BONUS SECTION: A VIEW BEHIND THE DOOR OF A PASTOR'S HOME

FOREWORD

by Dustin Woodward

I have been a pastor's kid my entire life. For all my thirty-six years, church and ministry have been intricately intertwined with all aspects of our lives as a family. You may read that statement and think it sounds odd, or you may feel sorry for me, but I would ask that you choose to feel neither.

I loved being a pastor's kid. Sure, there were ups and downs. Sure, there were negative people who said things they shouldn't have. Sure, there were times I felt like I had to share my parents with people, but can honestly say that I loved it all. Somehow, in the middle of all the craziness of growing up in ministry, my parents found a rhythm that worked well for our family. They seemed to always be at our games and school functions, and even when I watched my dad walk out the door during dinner to visit someone in the hospital who needed him, I knew we were still his priority. It was the way he got on the ground and played with my brothers and me when we were little. It was the way he treated my mom. It was the way he looked us in the eye when we were talking.

My dad has this way of being fully present wherever he is. It's comforting and reassuring. He may have been the church's pastor, but he was always my dad. He was just "dad" wherever we were; no matter who he was talking to or whatever meeting he was in.

The way my parents modeled pastoring opened my heart to easily say "yes" to God when He called me to ministry at the age of sixteen. I wanted to be a pastor like my dad, because I wanted to be a man like my dad. He's my hero.

After forty years of my dad and mom leading our church, my dad passed me the baton and I'm now the Lead Pastor of Citizen Church. Serving my parents in the roles of youth and associate pastor over the last fourteen years has been the joy of my life, and I am living the dream God gave me twenty years ago.

To say it is a privilege to work with my dad would be a massive understatement. Has it been perfect? No. Have we had disagreements? Yes. Has he had to correct me? Yes. But no matter what was going on and no matter what we were facing, he never stopped looking at me in the eye and saying, "I'm so proud that you're my son. You're my best friend. I believe in you. And I love you so much!" That made the difference in my life!

Time goes by so fast, and how you balance life, marriage, children, and ministry matters so much. In this book, my dad opens up about what life was like with our family in the middle of all the craziness. He talks about how to create those moments that stand out with your children, just like the moments in my life that I mentioned earlier. My dad wasn't perfect. But, he's close, and I'm not just saying that. To me, my dad represents peace, comfort, stability, kindness, courage, strength, support, and godliness. He is absolutely my best friend in the world.

I now have four kids of my own, and I have one goal: to be the dad to them that my dad has been to me. A dad that can say, "Follow me, as I follow Christ."

You're about to read a book that will change your life, if you let it. Open your mind to what God wants to show you. Let it soak in. Your children need you. They need you to be present, they need you to notice them, and they need to know they're your priority. Whatever your story is, and whether you view yourself as succeeding or failing at parenting, know that with God, the best is yet to come.

PREFACE

A Matter of Time

The fast pace of modern-day family life can make it easy to forget the simplicity of spending time with our children. Time is the most effective way to shape, mold, and prepare them to live in this world as a future influencer.

Our world desperately needs a generation of world-changers, those who understand that our society hangs in the balance of great spiritual stakes, and that a turning of the tide will only happen through those who are properly equipped.

As parents, we all intuitively understand the importance of spending time with our kids, but how can we make sure that we're spending quality time with them? How do we know that we're not occupying the same space, while focused on entirely different things, but actively engaging with our children and preparing them to lead their own generation?

There's an old story that's told about Picasso sitting in a park, when he was approached by a woman who asked him to make a portrait of her. He agreed, quickly drew her portrait, and handed it to the woman. She was very pleased.

She asked how much the portrait was, and Picasso reportedly told her it was $5,000. Taken aback, the woman tried to argue that it only took Picasso about five minutes to create. The rebuttal came quickly. It had taken Picasso's entire life.

Why is this story important? Most people view the value of time incorrectly.

> *If you desire someone's time, you're not desiring their current time, you're desiring the value of all their past time that went into making their current time desirable.*

This is exactly the way it is with our children. They desire our time. They want us more than anything in the world. Parents are desirable because of all the years of experience and all the roads that have been traveled. Parents have experienced all the ups and downs of life, all the joys and all the tears. It's taken a long time for us to get where we are and become who we've become.

Parents, you have a wealth of experience, wisdom, knowledge, and love to pass on, but you must carve out the time to give it to them.

Kairos Method

"Time" is one of the most common words in the English language. This one single word contains a broad variety of interpretations and meanings.

We track time by clocks and calendars that seem to rule our

lives. Time is constant and consistent, but time is anything but linear. In life, we all experience how time seems to speed up, slow down, or even stand still. Time may be linear but it's also very much alive providing us with all kinds of special moments.

The Greeks had two words for time. The first word, *chronos*, is defined as linear or sequential. It's measurable or quantifiable time. The second word, *kairos*, is defined as a season or an opportune time. It's understanding the value of a moment.

To clarify the difference of these two Greek words, think of *chronos* as the clock ticking second by second, and minute by minute. Think of *kairos* as the human element, that is, finding special moments in the middle of the ticking of the clock. Moments to give praise to your spouse, to hug a tear-stained toddler, or to have a meaningful conversation with your teenage son or daughter at a coffee shop. *Kairos* is not seconds and minutes, but moments of human connection that bring benefit to our lives, relationships, and families. The "*Kairos* Method" recognizes the untapped potential found in the small moments of time. It can be a smile, a nod, a kind word, a quick course-correct, listening attentively, or applauding loudly. All these are needed and craved by every family member. Stop for a moment and remember when you had one of those days when everything was going off the rails. Then, at the right moment, a friend gave you a few kind words, you received flowers from your husband, your child climbed up into your lap to cuddle, or your boss recognized you in front of all your coworkers. Those short *kairos* moments can powerfully re-energize you and give you the strength to go on. That is the wonder of *kairos*. It is a special moment that can reset someone's bad day. Every parent must hone their ability to take advantage of a *kairos* moment, in order to raise children who will change their world and the culture they live in.

The Apostle Paul states in Ephesians 5:15–16, "Look carefully then how you walk, not as unwise men but as wise, making the most of the time, because the days are evil" (Revised Standard Version).

When Paul instructs us to make the most of our time, he chooses the Greek word *kairos* to express this concept. This is the season or opportune time to act.

Paul views quality, and not necessarily quantity, as the important factor in time. He describes our time here on earth as a series of opportunities. We don't want to go through life with our head down, so focused on our own life and work, that we miss the daily opportunities to interject love, joy, wisdom, and life into our children.

Making the most of our *kairos* time is not about being passive, but about being proactive with every second that we have. Paul's mindset was to squeeze the most out of each second. What a great mindset to develop around family life! As you walk into the door of your house each day to greet your family, don't forget your *kairos* watch, reminding you to slow down and create moments that your children may never forget.

> *Time is free. Time is precious. Time is all you have. Master your time and you will master your life.*

INTRODUCTION

In the Beginning

K ay and I had been married for two and a half years, when an ordinary day became *the* day that started the greatest adventure of our lives.

As I walked into our house that day, Kay met me at the door with eyes sparkling and a huge smile, and she blurted out, "We're going to have a baby!" All in one moment I experienced shock, excitement, panic, laughter, tears, and the fun of telling our family and friends the good news.

A few days later when the dust settled from this celebratory news, I found myself alone to ponder what this meant. We were bringing a little human into a broken, sinful world where the devil desires to destroy anything resembling the image of God. Couple that with the weight of responsibility to love, guide, protect, and ultimately lead this child into a healthy and fulfilling life. Then I began to think the more important thoughts about where this child will spend eternity. I was completely overwhelmed.

In the next few years, we went on to have two more boys. Each time the news was equally exciting, but sobering too.

My desire was to be the best dad I could possibly be and to bring as much joy and fulfillment into their little lives as possible.

During all three pregnancies, I committed myself to pray for our unborn children every day. Each morning during those nine months, I would arrive at the church at 6 a.m. and walk into a dimly-lit auditorium to find my favorite spot. It was near the front, slightly to the left of the platform. On cold mornings, I would hover over the heater vent that was pouring out warm air, and there I prayed for our children that I had not yet met.

Increasingly, each morning I was keenly aware that God was in the process of creating and forming a little baby, while I was in the process of imagining who they would grow up to be. I have many fond memories of those early mornings, praying for them and trying to imagine what they would look like. Would it be a boy or a girl? Would they have blonde hair or brown hair? Would they have blue, green, or brown eyes? Would they look more like me or more like their mother, Kay?

There are many great experiences and adventures that life offers, but none can match watching the miraculous development of our own children.

Image Bearers

It is incredible to think that within seconds after a child is born, nurses, family, and friends will say, "Your baby looks just like you, or just like their mother. He's got your nose; she has your eyes." Their facial features will always resemble their parents somewhat, because our children are not only created in the image of God, but also created in our own likeness. They will not only look like us, but they will act like us, talk like us, and walk like us.

As parents, God gives us the responsibility of molding them into healthy, functioning adults, emotionally, socially, physically, and spiritually.

More importantly, as parents, we are the image-bearers of God. It states in Genesis 1:27–28a, "So God created mankind in his own image, in the image of God he created them; male and female he created them. God blessed them and said to them, 'Be fruitful and increase in number; fill the earth and subdue it.'"

The first commandment God gave was specifically to parents. It was to be fruitful and to multiply. God placed his image upon Adam and Eve. They carried and reflected the image of God.

> *If we do not reflect God's image, we are not fully equipped for parenthood.*

The greatest responsibility of parenthood is to lead our children to Jesus Christ. Our children's concept of God is more derived by our behavior than any other force in life. We will create a bridge or a barrier in our child's ability to understand God.

What we do right becomes effortless for our children to

believe about God. If we are generous, it's easy for them to believe God is generous to us. If we are faithful, it's easy for them to believe God is faithful. If we are moral, kind, and forgiving, they will tend to believe that about God.

Likewise, what we do wrong becomes easy for our children to believe about God. If we are verbally abusive, absent, aloof, legalistic, or stingy, they will naturally attribute those characteristics to the nature of God.

Imagine a young boy who comes home late for dinner one evening. Everyone had already filled their plates and started eating.

He quickly noticed all that was left was a slice of bread and a glass of water. His heart sank because he was so hungry! Suddenly he saw his father's hand reach across the table, pick up his empty plate, and replace it with the father's own full plate. That night his father had only a slice of bread and a glass of water. When that boy became a man, he realized that throughout his life he knew what God was like by what his father did that night.

> *We all bear an image of some kind, but this is a sobering question: whose image are you bearing?*

Fad Followers

The nine months of pregnancy goes by too fast for the preparation it takes for the new household addition. Plus, there is tremendous social and cultural pressure to do everything right according to the latest, greatest, or most popular fads. As parents, we certainly don't want to be out of touch or to be looked down on by not following what are considered best parenting practices.

I remember the enormous pressure Kay and I felt. Do we take birthing classes or not? Should we have a natural birth, or ask for every drug in the hospital? What about breastfeeding or formula, pacifier or no pacifier, co-sleeping or crib sleeping, disposable diapers or cloth diapers, pre-school, home school, public school, or private school? Sports or no sports, or how many sports? Spanking or no spanking?

We were faced with all these questions before our child was even born. It's exhausting trying to think through everything and desperately wanting to make the right decision, coupled with the fear of making the wrong decision and everyone viewing us as "bad" parents.

The Baby's Home

The day Kay and I came home from the hospital with our first son, I lugged into the house what I considered a bunch of foreign objects: a breast pump, car seat, diaper bag, bottles, formula, and a pacifier. While sorting through everything, for some reason, I couldn't find the instructional manual on how to raise our child. I couldn't find it anywhere in the hospital bags.

Why? Because there isn't one. Think about that. Raising kids is such an important, serious task, and yet there's no "how to" manual.

I'm sure most young dads like myself don't give fatherhood much thought until the day it happens. Up until that time I had never been around a baby, and I'm not sure I had even held a baby. The closest experience I'd had to having a baby was owning a dog, and that doesn't come close. I was totally lost, and had no idea what to do with this little creature.

When I bought a new car from the Ford dealership, they were very intentional on helping me to understand every detail of the car. They offered a three-hour training course, walking me through all the vehicle's functions, including how to operate the digital console screen. Additionally, the car came with an extensive owner's manual filled with minute details for quick access on every problem that might arise. But, there's no such luck when it comes to a manual for babies.

The day after we had our baby the hospital staff was working hard to get all the paperwork done for us to be discharged, because a whole new batch of expectant moms were arriving. They wheeled Kay and our baby to the front doors of the hospital in a wheelchair, helped her into the car, waved goodbye, and ran back in to deliver more babies.

We took that small little baby home with us, walked through the front door of our house, looked at each other, and said, "Now what?" And we have asked that question every day for the last twenty years.

> *Raising children is hard. Any parent who says differently is lying, or campaigning for a "Parent of the Year" award.*

Parenting is emotionally and intellectually draining, and it often requires personal or career sacrifices, not to mention serious financial challenges.

The federal government estimates that the average cost of raising a child to age eighteen exceeds $190,000. Now that's a thought that never crossed my mind when we were thinking about having a baby. Kids are needy, and extremely demanding of our time from the moment of birth to…well, maybe forever. Parenting is difficult on so many levels, but Christian parenting adds another dimension to the challenge.

It's the challenge of not only training and equipping them for life, but also passing on our faith to our kids amid peer pressure, media pressure, and the growing absence of godly examples. We are living in a society that is moving us quickly toward "freedom from religion," instead of "freedom of religion."

I vividly remember the moment I fully understood the war of choices that our kids face every day, and it frightened me. I was picking up our middle son, Jonathan, from football practice during his freshman year of high school. As I waited, I watched the other high school kids interact outside my car window.

A pretty girl walked out of the gym from cheerleading practice, and a group of guys started yelling inappropriate things at her. She gave them "the finger," but then walked up to the truck where they were sitting.

She leaned in seductively to whisper something in the boy's ear, and there was immediate laughter and arm punching. Tires spun and more cat calls were made. In that moment, I got a snapshot of everyday life in high school.

Helping our kids navigate this life is challenging, scary, and takes skillful training. We must see the full cost of what it means to be a parent. It's challenging and difficult on so many fronts. But, it is also a heroic and noble endeavor. It is a call for those willing to lay their life down and give the best they have.

> *Parenting will call for our best intelligence, our finest judgment, and our whole heart.*

Parenting requires the tough decision to say, "I will devote my best time and energy every day to this task which involves personal sacrifice." At the same time, it's one of the greatest and most rewarding adventures anyone will ever experience.

SECTION 1

The Words You Speak

"Sticks and stones may break my bones..." We've heard this silly nursery rhyme and laughed at it, but the all-too-real truth is that words can produce severe emotional and psychological damage. The good news is that words can also produce life, health, and growth. Children need to hear us speak words that will not only allow them to grow and survive, but to thrive in changing their world.

CHAPTER 1

Speaking the Language of Our Forefathers

One Sunday morning after one of our services, I was standing in the atrium talking with a couple who were telling me that they had moved here from Mexico and only spoke Spanish when they arrived.

They learned English after living in Albuquerque for several years. I asked if their kids were bilingual. To my surprise, they said, "No, we never speak Spanish in our home anymore."

The parents speak two languages fluently, but their children are rarely exposed to their parent's native language. The children are losing a part of their heritage simply because the parents are no longer speaking the language of their ancestors in their home.

There's an interesting story in the book of Nehemiah that explains this powerfully.

The Hebrew people had broken their covenant with God, and as a result, they willingly walked out from under His protective covering. The city of Jerusalem came under siege. It was burned and its walls were destroyed. Only a small remnant of people could still be found living amid the rubble.

As Nehemiah rode a donkey around the city assessing the challenge before him, he heard Hebrew children playing throughout the ravaged ruins. He noticed that they weren't speaking their native language. This is because the Hebrew men started marrying women of Ashdod, which was in direct disobedience of God's command. Their children spoke the language of Ashdod and could not speak the language of their Hebrew fathers.

Nehemiah was enraged by this discovery, because the loss of the language meant that the young Hebrews were losing their spiritual heritage. They now were speaking the language of another culture. The same thing is happening in Christian homes today.

A young generation is being raised that can't speak the spiritual language of their ancestors. Christianity has become their second language, while the culture of our time is their first language. Children are not hearing their parents declaring their faith, proclaiming the Word of God, and praying bold prayers.

> *If we do not model this language in our homes, our children will find it nearly impossible to be spiritually fluent themselves.*

The children in our homes will speak the language that they hear spoken.

Matthew 12:35–37 is a passage that has always captivated

me, "A good man brings good things out of the good stored up in him, and an evil man brings evil things out of the evil stored up in him. But I tell you that everyone will have to give account on the day of judgment for every empty word they have spoken. For by your words you will be acquitted, and by your words you will be condemned."

We are reminded that our words carry such tremendous power that one day we will be held accountable for the harm or blessing we have produced in others. This is a sobering thought. We can never be careless when it comes to the words we speak, but we must use them well.

This generation has adopted the language of their culture and has not been taught to communicate at a spiritual level. But, this is contrary to what God's Word instructs us to do as parents who are to teach the younger generation.

Deuteronomy 6:4–7 states,

> Hear, O Israel: The Lord our God, the Lord is one. Love the Lord your God with all your heart and with all your soul and with all your strength. These commandments that I give you today are to be on your hearts. Impress them on your children. Talk about them when you sit at home and when you walk along the road, when you lie down and when you get up.

This instruction was given to parents that they might speak the Word of God to their children four times a day:

- when they are going to bed at night
- when they get up in the morning
- as they are sitting around the house
- when they are going somewhere.

These are not four random times but very specific, intentional ones. When we're busy working hard and our minds are engaged is not when we battle temptation.

Attacks come when we are inactive.

Think about those times. Often, they are late at night, early in the morning, when we are sitting around and hanging out, or when we are simply driving around. These are the times we are bombarded with fear, worry, lust, and wrongful desires. We cannot remove thoughts, but we can speak the Word of God that has power over temptation.

We must teach our children to speak and declare the Word of God. For example, we should teach them to speak to the enemy this way:

- If you come against me with debilitating fear, I come against you with scripture.
- If you come against me with worry and failure, I come against you with God's promises.
- If you come against me with lust, I come against you with the Word of God.

Moses gives us wise counsel in Deuteronomy. As parents, we should deliberately speak the Word of God and teach it to our children. Then our children will not only speak it, but also use it as a weapon to overcome the attacks of the enemy.

Parents, your voices release love, prayer, and praise. With your voice, you proclaim the plans and purposes of God.

Another great story I love is about coach Vince Lombardi. During a practice session for the Green Bay Packers, things were not going well for the team. Lombardi singled out one big guard for his failure to give his best.

It was a hot, muggy day when the coach called his guard aside and verbally unloaded on him. He called him out for not blocking, tackling, or trying his hardest. The big guard dropped his head and walked into the locker room.

Forty-five minutes later, when Lombardi walked in, he saw the big guard sitting in front of his locker still wearing his uniform. His head was bowed, and he was sobbing quietly. Vince Lombardi could be gruff and very demanding, but he was also referred to as the compassionate warrior.

He walked over to his football player and put his arms around his shoulder. Lombardi continued to tell him that he wasn't doing his best, but that was not the end of the story. Lombardi assured him that he would stick with him until he became a great football player.

The big guard, Jerry Kramer, straightened up and felt a great deal better. As a matter of fact, he went on to become one of the all-time greats in football and was recently voted to the all-time team for the first fifty years of professional football.

The power of the human tongue is extremely potent. It's the power to transform another human being. But think about this: if human words can have that much power and influence in our lives, what kind of power could God's words have in our lives?

To fully understand the power of our words, we must go all the way back to Genesis 1:3, "And God said, 'Let there be light.'" God spoke into existence that which did not exist. This chapter emphasizes the phrase, "And God said." In verse 6, "And God said." In verse 9, "And God said." In verse 11, "Then God said." In verse 14, "And God said." In verse 20, "And God said." In verse 24, "And God said."

Each time God spoke, he created something. God spoke into existence something that did not exist. In this passage, we find that the power of God flows from his words.

When God created us in his likeness, he created a reflection, an optical counterpart. He did not reproduce himself so we might be little gods. But he did the next best thing. He created us with the ability to reason, to plan, to dream, and to choose.

> *I'm convinced that the core of being made in God's image is the power to create things with our words.*

What a thought! Humankind has the ability to open our mouths and speak that which does not exist into existence.

CHAPTER 2

Please Just Speak a Blessing

One Sunday morning after church, I was in the lobby visiting with people. Before locking up the building, I walked back into the auditorium to grab my notebook. I looked over and saw a guy still sitting on the front row. I walked over and introduced myself to him.

I instantly detected that he had experienced something from God that morning and he was in no hurry to leave. He said, "Thank you for your sermon series on the family for the last few weeks. It literally changed my life!"

I sat down next to him and said, "Tell me about it."

He started by telling me that he had grown up in a very dysfunctional home. His dad was an alcoholic, with an explosive and violent temper.

He said, "I grew up in a home with constant screaming and cursing mixed with physical violence. Every day of my life he told me that I'm a loser, a deadbeat, an embarrassment to him, and I would never amount to anything. He constantly told me that I had ruined his life.

"When I was sixteen, he kicked me out of the house. I haven't seen him since, and I swore I would never see him again. But after hearing your messages on the family, I knew I had to go back home and at least try to find healing from the deep-rooted hatred and resentment I've carried against my father. After hearing you speak, I wanted so desperately to experience what your children did when you laid your hands upon them and prayed a blessing over them.

"A couple of weeks ago, I drove all the way to where my father still lives. I walked up to the house where I grew up and instantly was overcome by a flood of painful memories. Standing on the porch, I took a deep breath to calm my nerves and knocked on the door.

"My father stepped to the screen door and without opening it, the first thing he said to me after all those years was, 'What kind of problem did you get into that you need me to bail you out of? You wouldn't be here unless you needed money.

"As I stepped into the house I said, 'Dad, I don't need money. I don't need you to bail me out of any trouble. I just want to talk to you about something. After all these years, I have nothing to show for myself. I feel like I'm dying on the inside. I have nothing and nobody in my life. I hate myself, I hate what I have become, and I'm exactly what you told me I would be: a no-good loser. The reason why I've come all this way is to tell you that something remarkable has happened in my life. I started going to church and I've accepted Jesus Christ into my life. It's opened my eyes and has given me hope for the future that I've never had. I've come all this way to ask you to do one thing for me. I need you to speak life-giving words over me. I want you to speak a blessing over my life! I know it may not make any sense to you but I don't feel like I can continue in life without it. It doesn't have to be long. It can be a word, a phrase, a sentence. I just need you to say something positive about me.

"There was absolutely no response from my dad. He walked down the hallway and into his bedroom. I could hear him pacing back and forth, and eventually he made his way back into the living room where I was standing.

"After what seemed to be an eternity of awkwardness and total silence, I could tell he wanted to say something, yet nothing came out of his mouth. As I stood there I realized the reason for his silence. He could not think of one positive thing to say about me. Not one good thing came to mind. He finally walked slowly toward me and put his hand on my shoulder but spoke nothing. While he stood there in complete silence with his head down, I noticed that he was crying. His tears fell from his face as I saw them splatter on my shoe.

"He finally broke the silence and said, 'Son, I really do love you. I'm so sorry and I do believe there is greatness inside of you.'"

He concluded, "Those words, out of an unholy man, were like a holy anointing that poured over me. When I walked out of his house, I felt like a different man."

As I sat and listened to his story, I think for the first time in my life I fully understood the scripture found in Proverbs 18:21, "The tongue has the power of life and death, and those who love it will eat its fruit."

In the book of Genesis, there is a story where Isaac blesses his son Jacob. Genesis 27:27–29 states,

> So he went to him and kissed him…he blessed him and said… "May God give you heaven's dew and earth's richness—an abundance of grain and new wine. May nations serve you and peoples bow down to you. Be lord over your brothers, and may the sons of your mother bow down to you. May those who curse you be cursed and those who bless you be blessed."

Blessings are found throughout the Bible. God blessed Moses. The Priest blessed Joshua. The Patriarchs blessed Jesus. Jesus blessed the bread, disciples, and children.

The last thing Jesus did on this earth was bless the people on the day He ascended into Heaven. Luke 24:50 reads, "When he had led them out to the vicinity of Bethany, he lifted up his hands and blessed them."

Hebrews 11:20 expounds on the blessing Isaac gave to Jacob by using a specific phrase, "By faith Isaac blessed Jacob..." Notice a father is speaking forth something by faith that does not yet exist.

A blessing is speaking something over our children strictly by faith and expecting to see it happen in their lives.

Name Tags

I watched my son, Dustin, do something brilliant with his son, Asher. When Asher was in third grade, there were a couple of boys in his class that were picking on him and calling him names. It began affecting him to the point that school became a place of dread and pain for him. The boys were relentless with their bullying.

Dustin sat down with Asher one afternoon to talk about what they were calling him and how it made him feel. Dustin's heart broke as he could see how this bullying affected Asher's self-worth. Later that day, Dustin went to the store and bought a package of name tags and a magic marker.

Every morning when Asher got out of bed, Dustin had a name tag waiting on him at the dining room table. Each day he wrote out a new name to stick on Asher's shirt. Dustin wrote names such as "Warrior," "Champion," "Creative," "Brilliant," and "Leader." Asher would wear the name tag all morning and take it off as he was getting out of the car to walk into school. The last thing Dustin would say to him as he peeled off his name tag was, "Remember who you are. It doesn't matter what anybody else says, it only matters what I say. You are a CHAMPION!"

That one small act changed everything about Asher's school experience. Instead of going into school believing a lie about himself, he walked in believing who his dad said he was. The power of doing something that small is stunning.

It's the simple power of WORDS!

This is exactly what God will do for each of us as we enter our heavenly home. Revelation 2:17 reminds us, "...to the one who is victorious...I will also give that person a white stone with a new name written on it, known only to the one who receives it."

God has a secret and personal name that He calls you. On the day you stand in front of your mighty God, He will reveal that name to you. This name is who you will be throughout eternity. I can't wait to hear the name my Heavenly Father has reserved for me. In the same way, your children long and love to hear the name you have given them. By our words we can bless or curse, bring life or death, produce healing or destruction.

The Most Valuable Moment of the Day

When our kids were young, it was our habit to tuck each of them into bed. The days seemed long and by bed time, we often felt exhausted. However, we viewed this valuable moment as non-negotiable. We developed a nightly standard, so we wouldn't simply get our kids in bed and miss something powerful.

I would sit on the edge of the bed with our oldest son, Dustin, and ask, "Do you know what your name means? Dustin means warrior, it means champion!" I would lay my hand on him and say, "You are a warrior and a champion for the Kingdom of God. You will rise up and lead, instead of following others.

You are a world changer. You are bold and courageous. You will influence the nations! God has created you with power and wisdom."

Then I would pray over him. I wouldn't pray a cute memorized children's "night-night" prayer but a bold, audacious prayer. I'd ask God to send angels to watch over him and protect him, but I'd take it a step further. Parents, pray for more than blessings and protection. Pray for your children to grow in wisdom. Pray they would experience the fullness of Christ. Pray for their friendships to be healthy and positive. Pray for their future spouse. Pray for yourself to have wisdom to guide them.

After praying with Dustin, I'd walk into Jonathan and Brandon's room, and sit down on the side of the bed with Jonathan. I'd ask him, "Do you know what your name means? Jonathan means God's gift. Jonathan, you are a gift to this world. You are blessed by God, and you will be successful in everything you touch. You will be known as a faithful and loyal friend. You will be loved by all. People will be blessed by simply knowing you. You will make the world a better place to live in." Then I would lay my hand on him and pray over him.

Then I'd walk over to Brandon's bed and sit down. I'd again ask, "Brandon, do you know what your name means? It means beacon of light, a lighthouse. Brandon, you will grow up to be a bright light in this dark world. You will never lose your way in life because of the clarity of God's light that shines in you. You will be a great light that people will follow. They will follow you and not even know why. People of all kinds will be

attracted to you and what you say. You are a world changer!"
Then I would lay my hand on him and pray over him.

Now years later, I have the privilege of seeing the impact
of repeatedly speaking faith, life, success, and direction over
my sons each night. What I spoke over them as small children
is exactly who they are as grown men. It is stunning for me to
see how each one has become the person who I declared them
to be. They heard it and they believed it.

Dustin is a spiritual warrior for the Kingdom of God. He is
known across the country as a strong leader who is wise beyond
his years. He's already positioned to have a national influence.

Everyone who knows Jonathan agrees that he is a gift to
anyone who connects to him. He's one of the kindest people
you will ever meet. He's loyal, faithful, and generous. He has
an extraordinary love for God and his Church. He is a Doctor
of Pharmacy and is highly successful in his field.

People are attracted to Brandon like bugs to light. He is a
human lighthouse. While still young, he leads one of the largest
college and young adult ministries in the country. People of all
kinds and backgrounds are attracted to his leadership. Brandon
is a light in a dark world.

In extreme detail, they are living out today what I boldly
spoke over them as young children.

Paul speaks about the gift of prophecy in 1 Corinthians
14:3, "But the one who prophesies speaks to people for their
strengthening, encouraging and comfort." These words of
edification and encouragement are spoken by the prompting
of the Holy Spirit.

A great example of this is found in Ezekiel 37. In a vision, Ezekiel sees himself standing in a desert. As far as he can see are bones and human remains. God asks Ezekiel in verse 3, "Son of man, can these bones live?" Ezekiel replies that only God knows. Then in verse 5 God says, "Prophesy to these bones and say to them... 'you will come to life.'" Ezekiel prophesies and the bones join together, flesh reappears, and they come back to life. A great army rose and stood before him.

As godly parents, we are to prophesy over our children. I know that the word prophesy has been misused and abused, and many people are turned off by it. Don't let the misuse scare you from experiencing one of God's great gifts. Prophesying is simply speaking life and encouragement over your children. It's declaring by faith that God will work mightily in them.

We know damage is caused when children grow up in a home of harsh words, name calling, and criticism. Words spoken to them repeatedly will negatively alter their destiny and haunt them the rest of their lives. But know this: when you speak life and success over your children, they begin to believe it. Your voice and your prayers for them activate the power of God in your kids.

I believe the greatest tragedy of our failure to pray is that an army of ministering angels is never dispatched from heaven on behalf of our kids. Remember, Jesus prayed and the angels ministered to him. Paul prayed in a storm, and an angel came to him on the ship. The church prayed for Peter, and an angel showed up to deliver him from prison.

Parents, pray that God will send warring angels to walk

with your children every day. Your voice activates heaven and puts the supernatural into action. Scripture reminds us we have not because we ask not.

Often as my kids got out of the car and began walking toward the entrance of their school, I sat there praying, "God send warring angels to walk beside them today, as they walk the halls, as they sit in classrooms, as they eat with their friends at lunch." I would pray over them until they left my sight.

Don't let a day go by without speaking a blessing over each member of your family. Positive, encouraging, kind, and loving words will properly mold and shape the people in your home.

SECTION 2

Four Foundations Every Parent Must Master

Foundations are critical to the success of every building. If a foundation is unstable or has cracks, the entire building will be compromised. Likewise, the foundation that parents build in their children is vitally important. Each parent must master these four foundational principles to set their children up for success.

CHAPTER 3

Foundation 1 – Leadership

One of the fondest memories I have of my parents was the day I left home for college. I said goodbye to my parents while standing in our driveway. My car was packed to the brim. Mom handed me a box filled with warm chocolate chip cookies she had just pulled from the oven. I hugged them both, and my dad could tell things were about to get emotional.

He said, "Hey, this is the most exciting day of your life. What a day! What an adventure!"

As I drove away leaving them standing there, I remember thinking, "I want to be just like my dad." What would cause an eighteen-year-old kid to have such a deep desire to be like his parents? The answer: living a life your kids respect and admire.

Parents who are leaders will raise children who become leaders.

The only training I had in raising a family is what I experienced growing up and watching how my mom and dad raised me and my brothers. When we enter parenthood, the first question we must seriously ponder is this, "Do I want more 'mini-me's' running around, because that is exactly what I'm going to produce?" Children do what we do. It's like the old saying, "Like father, like son."

Like Father, Like Son

It was July 1, 1898, and the Spanish-American War was in full swing. At the bottom of San Juan Hill, Lt. Col. Teddy Roosevelt strapped on his boots and led his Rough Riders regiment up the hill under fierce Spanish gunfire, and on to victory. For his courage, he was awarded the Congressional Medal of Honor.

On June 6, 1944 in Normandy, France during World War II, while sitting on a transport ship, Gen. Teddy Roosevelt Jr. prepared to attack the heavily fortified coast. Teddy Roosevelt Jr. requested to lead the D-Day invasion, and at first, his superiors denied his request, "You're fifty-seven years old. No other general is going ashore with the first wave of troops."

Roosevelt insisted, "It will steady the men to know I'm with them." So, Teddy Jr. strapped on his boots and led the charge onto the beach under fierce German gunfire, and on to victory. For his courage, he was awarded the Congressional Medal of Honor, just like his father had received. Roosevelt had instilled in his four boys a sense of duty, courage, and a willingness to lead. The legacy of each generation is the level of leadership that has been passed on to them.

> *The leadership traits we pass down cannot happen without large measures of time, patience, and love!*

Everyone dreams of their child becoming a great leader of the future: whether president of the United States, CEO of a multinational corporation, professional athlete, world-famous musician, or even a pastor with a global influence.

Seeing a child grow up to become important and successful is something every parent wants, but raising leaders isn't an exact science. Every child is unique. Yet, we have guidelines in the form of biblical principles that cover all children. These principles enhance and supersede personality temperaments, generational challenges, and weaknesses.

This is something I've thought about for many years. Why are we as Christian parents, empowered by the Holy Spirit, not producing an army of extraordinary leaders? I think it's due to an absence of intentional leadership.

Not all parents are leaders, but all are in a leadership position, and as such, can develop leadership skills within their children. Some children may display more confidence and leadership traits than others, but it doesn't necessarily make them a leader. It has been proven throughout history that anyone can learn to be a leader.

As a parent, you will play a huge part in whether your child is a leader or follower. You can help them discover who God created them to be, discover how to treat others, and discover how they should act.

Personally, I want my sons to be responsible, kind, and

loving. I want them to treat everyone, from the CEO to the janitor, with the same level of respect and compassion. Those traits aren't going to happen by themselves. They must be learned, and if they must be learned, then we must teach them.

Being a leader does not necessarily mean that a person is simply telling others what to do. One of the most important traits of a leader is the ability to set a personal standard of behavior for others to follow.

As a parent, ask yourself these questions: "Do you want your child to be a leader or a follower? Do you want them to be confident or insecure? Do you want them leading their friends at school or their school friends leading them? Do you want them to be exceptional or average?" Many parents seem to be content with average, but that is not for me or my children. The dictionary defines average as common or ordinary.

> *The last thing God called us to be is common.*

I would not take it as a compliment if someone said to me, "I view you as an average father, an average husband, and an average public speaker." I would be horrified to hear those words.

We were not created to be average and blend in with everybody else. We were created to live an extraordinary life. The responsibility greatly rests on our shoulders as parent-leaders for our children to live at that level.

After Kay and I were married, we enjoyed going back to Alabama to visit her parents. I remember getting up early and smelling the aroma of breakfast cooking. Kay's mom was famous for her homemade, made-from-scratch biscuits. They were by far the best biscuits I've ever had. The ingredients she used were staples found in most kitchens: flour, salt, baking powder, milk, and shortening. However, the artistry resided not in the individual ingredients, but in the skillful combination of those ingredients. The outcome was magnificent.

In the same way, raising influential leaders is a lot like making delicious biscuits. We have everything we need. We simply need to learn to skillfully combine and instill the right traits. In fact, I believe only a few critical elements are required to shape our children into cultural leaders. However, like any premier biscuit baker, parenting is knowing when and how to combine those leadership ingredients to ultimately produce powerful influencers.

Two hundred years ago, settlers wandering across the Midwest were faced with many challenges. One of the leading causes of death among children was poison from snake bites. Rattlesnakes and copperheads were in abundance.

When the settlers found a place to stake their claim and build their new home, occasionally they would do so unaware that the area was infested with snakes. The danger of snakes had become such a threat to settlers that they became very intentional in building their homes above the snake line. At a certain elevation, poisonous snakes cannot survive. Safety came by being on higher ground. It was nature's invisible, yet very real, line that provided protection to those who abided by it. Similarly, there is a very real spiritual line of safety that comes as we live our lives at a higher spiritual elevation.

Here's an example of how we can turn routine moments into teaching opportunities that will help form our children and give them truths they will never forget.

You can be sitting in a restaurant with your thirteen-year-old drawing on a napkin. This works best when it's off the cuff, and everyone is in a good mood. Draw a horizontal line and write on top of the line "Above People" and write underneath the line "Below People." Explain to them that our brain is programmed to live below the line. It's naturally where we gravitate. We must reprogram our way of thinking to live above the line.

As you start writing on the napkin or scrap piece of paper, think of characteristics of people who live above the line, and do the same with those who live below the line. Then let your child help you list traits on both sides of the line. This is a powerful visual that will help them see what produces success and what produces failure. This can be as elementary or intellectually deep as you desire.

Many corporate executives use this to elevate business success among their teams by helping them think at a higher level. From a young age, our children need to be taught how not to follow the average-thinking process of everyone around them, but to push themselves above the line in all areas of life, whether academically, socially, or spiritually.

Shamgar, the Not-So-Ordinary Farmer

Many great men are mentioned throughout the Old Testament. But, there is an account of one man that is only forty-six words long, and his life is an example to all of us.

The account of Shamgar, an ordinary farmer who becomes one of the judges of Israel, is told in four verses in 1 Chronicles 4, and Judges 3 and 5. The story takes place at a very chaotic time in history. It was such a difficult time that Judges 5:6 states, "In the days of Shamgar son of Anath, in the days of Jael, the highways were abandoned; travelers took to winding paths." Judges 21:25 gives an overview of those days, "In those days Israel had no king; everyone did as they saw fit." This is very descriptive of the present day.

People no longer felt safe to travel main roads. Instead they were taking back roads and hidden pathways, trying to stay out of sight of thieves and robbers. The nation of Israel had completely lost control of law and order. It was overrun by thugs, thieves, and murderers. People even had to carefully walk around the outer edges of cities to find an entry point without being robbed or killed. Many lived in fear, stopped traveling, and hid in their houses. But along comes Shamgar.

Judges 3:31 reads, "After Ehud came Shamgar son of Anath, who struck down six hundred Philistines with an ox-goad. He too saved Israel."

Shamgar was nothing more than an ordinary farmer who owned an ox-goad. This farming tool was a long eight-foot-pole with a sharp end on it. The other end was flat, serving as a chisel or pry-bar. When the oxen became sluggish, the farmer would goad them to get them moving again.

Shamgar was not a military man. He was not a politician. He was not a city leader. He was a farmer. But, Shamgar didn't wait until he became great to do something great. He didn't wait on someone else to fix the problem. He didn't ask someone to do something about their out-of-control nation. Shamgar got up and did something, saving his nation. He may have been an ordinary farmer, but he was an extraordinary leader. The right ingredients, skillfully combined in any ordinary person, will produce a leader like Shamgar! We can glean two leadership principles to teach our kids from this amazing story.

Don't Make Excuses

Leaders don't make excuses. Life may not be what you hoped or wanted. Maybe you're not where you thought you would be by this time in life. Maybe life has dealt you a bad hand. Maybe you didn't have a positive role model as a child. Maybe you've made mistakes in your life, in your marriage, with your kids, or with your finances. I understand that! But, what are you going to do about it?

One of the reasons why there are so many ineffective Christians in our nation is because people are waiting for someone else to do something. We often hear people say, "Somebody in charge needs to do something!"

> *But the only person capable of changing your future is you.*

When Shamgar saw that the roads were shut down because of thieves and murderers, he realized it would keep him from selling his harvest. It threatened any kind of successful future that he wanted. In fact, the whole nation was being threatened. Shamgar decided to do something about it. He didn't wait until he had the right weapon, or a position of leadership, or an army to back him up. He decided to do something with the resources he had at his disposal. All he owned was an ox-goad.

> *Never let your circumstances limit you or God. You have more than enough to accomplish God's plan for your life.*

Moses merely had a staff, but it opened the Red Sea. David merely had a slingshot, but it delivered a nation from the Philistines. Samson merely had a donkey's jawbone, but he killed one thousand enemy soldiers with it. One little boy merely had two fish and five loaves of bread, but it fed five thousand people.

Children need to know they shouldn't make excuses because God has given them all the right ingredients. The main ingredient is the dynamic power of the Holy Spirit. Mix that into anything that needs to be done, and it will surely succeed. God doesn't call the equipped, he equips the called.

We Advance One Step at a Time

Shamgar killed six hundred men. How is this possible? He did it one at a time. We lose weight one pound at a time. We write a book one chapter at a time. We advance to the championship game one game at a time. Shamgar targeted and eliminated one threat at a time.

Parents, convey to your children that most people will look at insurmountable challenges and decide to do nothing, waiting on somebody else to do something. Teach and tell them, "The only somebody is you." Shamgar saved a nation when he used what he had.

When it comes to greatness, we can't focus on not being smart enough, fast enough, good-looking enough, or strong enough to achieve what we desire. It doesn't matter what people think or what people say.

Jesus said in John 14:12, "...whoever believes in me will do the works I have been doing, and they will do even greater things than these..."

Your children are destined for greatness!

As stated before, being a leader does not necessarily mean that a person is in a position to tell others what to do. Many of the most powerful or influential leaders in history influenced millions or even entire generations simply by making powerful individual choices. Some of the most important traits a leader must have are the ability to make right decisions, stand up to peer pressure, and set a personal standard of behavior.

Four Qualities Every Leader Needs

As Kay and I were raising our three boys, we wanted to instill specific qualities into their characters to help them to make wise decisions and give them courage to be leaders.

"I Can" Attitude

Leaders understand there will be many people who will tell them what they cannot do or why they cannot be something. Leaders stay focused on maintaining a positive attitude no matter what the people around them say or do. Leaders stand up to peer pressure every day to make choices for themselves. This is why it's important to teach your children to say "Yes, I can!" even when they are not sure. Help them understand the power of a positive attitude.

It is natural for every child who is confronted with something challenging to say, "I can't." It may be natural, but it's not productive. Those simple words have caused millions to not reach their potential in life. What a shame to be stopped by such simple words, "I can't."

Saying "I can't" is often an excuse not to try. It makes giving up easy. Help kids find the "I can" in every life challenge.

When our boys were small, every time I heard them say, "I can't," I would say, "There once were two boys. One would say, 'I can't,' and the other would say, 'I can,' and they were both right!"

> *What we believe about ourselves is how we will live our lives.*

Don't let your kids develop negative "I can't" attitudes. Remind them that the Bible teaches us in Philippians 4:13, "I can do all this through [Christ] who gives me strength."

We can raise children to be negative or positive, and we know which one will succeed at the higher level.

Perseverance

Every leader must have this trait. It is easy to quit when facing something difficult in life. While it is harder to persevere, it is more rewarding. Quitting is easy. It's a habit that begins at a young age.

As a student pastor for twelve years, I watched the same

scene play out repeatedly in many families. Teenagers would tell their parents that they wanted to quit a certain sport or activity because a teacher didn't like them, a coach was being unfair, or the other kids were being mean. Often, the parents allowed them to quit. Once that negative pattern is established in our children, it will most likely be a trait they carry the rest of their lives.

We had a slogan in our house that our kids knew well, "Woodwards Never Quit!" If they felt a teacher or coach was being unfair with them, they knew to go directly to that person to resolve the issue.

They knew our stance: we were not going to step in every time they had a social crisis with a peer or a conflict with an authority figure. We expected them to do their best to resolve it. Quitting the team or changing schools was never an option simply because someone was mean to them or they thought they were being treated unfairly.

As Kay and I taught this basic social skill of conflict resolution, we were firm, but not rigid. There were times we stepped in on behalf of our children to help them deal with a situation that was beyond their maturity level. That's what parents do, but balance is required.

One of my favorite movies is *The Blind Side*. This movie is based on the true story of Leigh Anne Tuohy, a wealthy socialite in Memphis, who takes a homeless black teen, Michael Oher, into her home. With the support from his new family, he becomes a professional football player.

My favorite scene in the movie is when the actress, Sandra Bullock, who plays Leigh Anne, watches her son Michael at football practice. The coach is frustrated because Michael lacks aggressiveness and is not effectively hitting and blocking. Leigh Anne disagrees with how the coach is handling the situation.

So, she marches onto the football field in the middle of practice in her high heels, grabs Michael by the shoulder pads, and begins instructing him on how and what to do. She adjusts some other players as well. As she's walking off the field, she walks by the coach, whose name is Burt, and says, "You can thank me later."

Short pause. "Burt, it's later."

I laugh every time I see that scene.

If you want to know what my wife Kay is like, this describes her perfectly! She's a southern belle with southern charm who is not intimidated by anyone.

When our kids were playing football, Jonathan had a coach that was probably the most intense man I've ever known. The first time I saw him was at a parents' orientation meeting at the beginning of the season. This large man, complete with a big, black mustache spoke with a deep, gruff voice that commanded everyone's attention.

The theme of his talk that night was "stupid parents." He went down a list of ten things stupid parents do, starting each phrase with, "You are a stupid parent if you..."

I stood there with my mouth wide open and in total shock at what I was hearing. He ran this little league team like a professional football team. In the next few years, our little league team won the national championship two years in a row in Las Vegas. A couple of years later, our son's high school won the state championship three years in a row under the same coach.

He had one goal: to win. In all those years, I avoided him like the plague. He had this unique way of making you feel like an idiot if you dared ask him a question or make a comment! I have never met anyone so intimidating in my life.

One of his rules was that a player could never miss practice. No one dared challenge that. Well, we had a problem. Wednesday nights were our student ministry night at the church, and that was a top priority for us. That was non-negotiable in our family. One night at practice, Kay and I knew we had to tell the coach that our son had to leave practice thirty minutes early every Wednesday.

We were standing under a tree arguing about how this conversation was going to go, and I was telling her that this is going to be a terrible conversation. In the middle of our debate, she turned around and strutted onto the field. As I stood under the tree, I remember saying to myself, "Dear God, have mercy on her soul." I watched at a far and safe distance as she approached the coach. I could see her talking at a rapid speed like she normally does. As she kept talking, she stepped toward the coach, and he took a step back. She continued to talk, taking another step forward, while he continued taking another step back. All the time he was nodding his head, "Yes."

Later, she recounted that she said, "Of course, this will not affect his playing time or go against him in any way, right? We are clear on that, correct?"

His response was, "Of course, Mrs. Woodward." She turned around and confidently marched off the field. She passed by me while I was still hiding behind the tree and said, "That's taken care of, and he'll never say another word about it."

Jonathan was a running back, but got little playing time and had never scored a touchdown. One afternoon as practice was starting, Kay and I were sitting in lawn chairs on the sidelines. Without notice, she marched onto the field again, zeroed in on this big, scary coach.

As she approached him she said, "Do you realize that every time we get the ball close to the goal line, you take Jonathan out of the game and put in the first-string player to score the touchdown. The next time we're close to the goal in a game, I want you to leave him in and give him a chance to score. Do you see any problem with that, because I don't? I want you to leave him in and give him a chance to score. And if you do, I will make you one of my famous chocolate cakes."

The next Friday night we were sitting in the stands at the football stadium. The game was in the fourth quarter, and our team had driven the ball all the way down to the five-yard line. The coach called "time out" and yelled Jonathan's name. He ran over to him and the coach said, "Jonathan, we are going to hand off the ball to you. I want you to run straight up the middle and score this touchdown."

Then he grabbed him by the face mask, pulled him close, and said in that gruff voice of his, "If you fumble the ball, see your mother up there in the stands? That's where you're going to be sitting for the rest of the game!" And Jonathan knew he was dead serious.

Jonathan was extremely nervous as he ran onto the field. He

got in position, the quarterback handed the ball off to him, he held on to that ball for dear life, and scored his first touchdown! It was a glorious night for all of us, and he never knew about the chocolate cake bribe. Some things are better left unsaid!

Through Kay's strong example, all three of our boys have learned to confront issues head on and take the initiative, instead of hoping things will work out on their own or avoiding problems and hard conversations. She taught them to stick it out, work it out, and fix it instead of running from it. That's perseverance.

Commitment

Do you ever commit to doing something and then say to yourself, "I'll do it later?" You may never get around to doing it later. This may happen in small ways while someone is young, but this can become an unintentional trait that negatively affects future success.

Unreliability starts with small actions that don't seem all that bad:

- We tell somebody we'll call them later and then don't.
- We put an item on a to-do list and don't complete it.
- We commit to doing something for someone else and don't follow through.

All of this might seem harmless if it occurs once or twice. But, little things done repeatedly have a big impact on our lives.

Every time a commitment is broken, it sends a message that what a person says can't be trusted, or that their word doesn't mean much. It prevents them from achieving their goals and eventually causes people to lose trust.

On the other hand, honoring your commitments gives power to your words. They mean something. Commitments can be defined as follows: "You do what you say you're going to do when you say you're going to do it." Despite its simplicity, there's great power to be found in sticking to your commitments. Like anything else in life, commitment takes practice. Here are some ways that will help our kids keep their commitments:

Teach Them to Say, "No"

One way to maintain integrity is to teach children not to commit to things they can't guarantee they'll follow through on. Say, "no," to everything that's not aligned with essential priorities. Every single day we're forced to choose between yes and no. When we say, "yes," to things we don't have time to do, we have set ourselves up to dishonor our word.

Teach Them to Stick to the Commitments Made to Themselves

Help them honor the commitments they've made to themselves academically, in athletics, with church activities, and in personal goals. Honoring the commitments they've made to themselves will produce a discipline that will make it much easier to honor the commitments they make to others.

Teach Them to Honor Their Commitments to Others

Once your child has learned to say, "no," and honor their commitments to themselves, they should honor the ones that they've made to others. Here are some simple examples of not honoring one's commitments:

- A person says he will clean up a mess he left behind, but he never does.
- A person promises to deliver something by a certain date, but doesn't show up.
- A person tells a friend they'll meet them at a certain time, but is forty-five minutes late.

When we say one thing but do another, say things we don't mean, or consistently break our word to others, we profoundly diminish our credibility. People begin to see us as untrustworthy and unreliable. They stop taking anything that we say seriously. They lose respect for us. People will go around us or ignore us instead of following us.

Excellence

Develop the spirit of excellence within your children. Doing our very best is a daily decision. It's easy to be average, but it takes a focused effort every day to do your best. It's an attitude. Leaders choose to do their best in everything they do. It's not about being better than other people; it's about challenging yourself to be your best.

Teach your children to strive for excellence without comparing themselves to others. Help them understand the importance of challenging themselves to do their best every day.

For instance, school assignments and projects produce great teaching moments. I loved helping our kids to be as creative as they could be. We would go to a craft store to get everything we needed for their project. The diorama was my favorite. It was a shoe box with a hole cut on one end. Through this hole, the teacher could look inside and see a land of dinosaurs that had been carefully created. I never allowed my sons to do things halfway, but I asked them to push themselves to create something of which they could be proud.

For many years, all three of our boys entered a pinewood derby competition. We would dream, design, and craft the best-looking cars possible. Again, I pressed them to take their time and develop the car of their dreams. I loved seeing the excitement and the fulfillment of the finished project.

Taking pride in one's work needs to begin at an early age so the spirit of excellence will be threaded throughout everything done in life. This should be common sense. Yet today, it's a rare breed of people who chose to perform at high levels of excellence.

When all three of our sons were teenagers, I often talked to them about setting goals for themselves to accomplish in their future career choices. Dustin and Brandon chose full-time ministry, and Jonathan chose to be a Doctor of Pharmacy.

I encouraged them to work extremely hard and set goals to hit by the age of thirty. I told them this would solidify a successful future for them.

One afternoon shortly after Dustin was hired as the student pastor at church, we were sitting in my office, along with another pastor. I was encouraging Dustin to work hard and develop himself into an exceptional speaker, and to be on the national stage by the age of thirty. I encouraged him to work on being invited to speak across the nation at churches, conferences, and seminars. I said to him, "If someone is going to lead, why not you? Make that happen by the age of thirty."

A little while later Dustin left the office, and the other pastor and I were still sitting there. I could tell something was bothering him. He opened his mouth to speak, hesitated for a moment, and then said, "Don't you think that's too much pressure to put on him? The pressure for him to be like you? The pressure to be a national speaker by the age of thirty? Don't you think that's a little presumptuous?"

My response to him was, "No, because I don't want him to measure up to me. I want him to surpass me. Yes, it's a lofty goal, but why should he shoot for anything less in life?"

Now, I'm not talking about the unrealistic expectations that come from perfectionism. There is a fine line between excellence and perfectionism. While perfectionism is the refusal to accept any standard that is less than perfect, excellence is the driving force that can teach our children how to shoot for goals beyond themselves.

Perfectionism can breed depression, anxiety, self-loathing, and other problems such as eating disorders or addictive behaviors. This can lead to a consistent dissatisfaction with a person's career, colleague, spouse, or even child. However, excellence is the mindset that allows our children to push themselves to success and self-fulfillment. We can help them accomplish this by not underestimating our children's intelligence, talents, and energy. We must allow God to show us everything our children can be, and not let our kids devalue themselves or settle into mediocrity.

For our three boys, it was paramount to set the age of thirty as a success marker. They used that marker to help them stay motivated, focused, and advancing toward their goals.

Now years later, Dustin and Brandon are recognized as national church speakers and leaders. The pharmacy Jonathan manages is recognized as having the highest ratings for all pharmacies in the region. My sons have all accomplished lofty goals while still under the age of thirty. Excellence breeds success, and success leads to self-fulfillment.

One important side-note to remember: success is wonderful, but it will still leave a person empty if God is not a part of life's equation.

We too often underestimate the intelligence, talent, and energy that flows through our children. They need parents who believe in them and will help them push the limits of excellence.

CHAPTER 4

Foundation 2 – Intentionality

W hen I was in my early thirties, I enjoyed playing golf. A couple of guys I played with were exceptional. Each time I went, they taught me something valuable that improved my game. The better I got, the more I wanted to play. I found myself thinking about golf all the time.

I watched professional golf tournaments on Sunday afternoons. I read golf magazines, and went to the golf store. I researched the newest and best golf clubs. I might have become more than a little obsessive.

One Saturday, I had just finished playing eighteen holes of golf. It was a beautiful, sunny day, and I'd had great fun with my friends. What was most satisfying was I had played one of my best rounds of golf.

I drove into our driveway, took my clubs out of the car, and walked in the front door. The moment I saw my wife I knew she'd had a rough morning with the kids. She looked tired, frustrated, and not at all happy with me. I stood there with three little boys clinging to my legs. All they wanted in life was my time and attention. Playing eighteen holes and a quick lunch had taken more than five hours of my Saturday.

I sat down on the couch, and all three began climbing on me. They couldn't get close enough and started fighting for my attention. That moment became one of the biggest reality checks of my life. On my day off, I had spent the best part of the day hitting a little ball down a fairway when I could have been investing in my three kids. It was one of those monumental moments of deep understanding, reminding me how much my kids needed me and how much I loved them.

Our sons are married: Dustin to Mandy, Jonathan to Jessica, and Brandon to Delaney. We consider them, and their wives, some of our closest friends. That should be the ultimate goal of every parent. Nothing will bring more enjoyment into your life than a life-long family bond that extends to grandchildren and great-grandchildren.

Not everyone enjoys that kind of legacy. Thanksgiving and Christmas are often when parents wish their relationship with their grown kids could be better. Sometimes the journey from authority figure to friend can be difficult, but if you can remember your goal, you will have clarity in the day-to-day grind.

It's in those daily activities where it's easy to get caught in the tide of work. By the time we get home, we don't have the energy to be intentional. We all go to bed at night. We all wake up every morning. We all eat. We all breathe. We all live in houses. We all have relationships. We fall into routines, and routines turn into what we consider normalcy. Our jobs give us money. Our friends give us companionship. Our families give us stability. Our cars give us mobility. Comfort and safety turn into complacency, and all of us are subject to falling into this pattern. Daily life just becomes automatic. We are allowing life to happen instead of making life happen.

It's vital that we live intentional lives. This doesn't mean that we are giving up on our routines. Rather, it means that we are intentionally inserting strategic habits into our routines.

The Habit Loop

Let's get scientific for a moment. There is an experiment that's done with rats to test their brain activity. Scientists place rats in a T-shaped maze and put some chocolate at the end of it. The first time the rats enter the maze, they sniff all the corners and eventually find the treat.

In the beginning, the rats show a lot of brain activity during the process of finding the treat. However, when the same rat was put into the maze repeatedly, researchers found a significant change in brain activity. By repeating the same test, rats' brain activity spiked at the beginning of the maze, and again at the end when they discovered the treat. The middle of the maze showed a significant decrease in brain activity. The rats knew the way to the end; it had become routine.

Our brains respond the same way. When an action becomes familiar, the automatic part of our brain kicks in, and we keep repeating the action. Essentially the brain goes into energy conservation mode. This neurological chain reaction is described as a "habit loop." We form continual habits, routines, and actions in our life without consciously calculating their outcome. Life becomes routine.

The more instinctive and automatic a response is, the less mental activity is going on. The more habitual something is, the less brain power is expended on the action. This is exactly what happens in our homes. Instead of being intentional in activities to improve our relationships, we get caught in the habit loop and keep repeating actions even if they are relationally destructive. We never calculate the negative results of our actions until it's too late.

Small, intentional decisions can drastically change any home, and will improve your family life. Parenting is one area that we can never allow complacency. We can't become brain-dead while at home, and expect our children to lead change in our culture.

Be Intentional in Your Parenting: Four Parenting Stages

Many family experts have written about the different stages parents encounter while guiding their kids into adulthood. Some divide it into three stages, others divide it into six stages, and a variety of names are given to describe each stage. Through my experience of parenting, I have discovered four distinct, clear stages. Being aware of each stage will help bring clarity to our parenting role. We must manage these four key leadership roles to properly prepare our children for their fast-approaching independence.

Be aware that the four phases will overlap each other, and different children will demand differing degrees of flexibility in moving from one phase to the next. This is not meant to be a cookie-cutter formula.

Phase One: Parents are Commanders (Ages One to Five)

In the first years of a child's life, a parent does practically everything for them. The parent functions as the commander-in-chief, telling the child who to listen to, what to eat, when to go to bed, or how to perform a task.

Within the first five years, many parents feel like they are solely disciplining their children twenty-four seven. Parents are tired, weary, and constantly second guessing themselves: "Am I right? Am I wrong? Am I doing the right things? Am I overboard on discipline?" We feel like we say, "No," a thousand times a day while our children ask us, "Why," a thousand times a day.

Now that I have the perspective of a grandparent, I realize that as a parent I made too big of a deal over small issues. We as parents should narrow the focus of our discipline to what is most important. Three important things should never be tolerated:

Disobedience / Dishonesty / Disrespect

Beyond that, don't sweat the small stuff. It's not that big of a deal if our kids knock over a glass of water on accident while at dinner. Of course, it makes a mess and can be frustrating, but it's not worth becoming angry and upset. Kids are clumsy, and so were we when we were kids. Simply clean it up and move on.

For those parents who feel overwhelmed with small children, the best encouragement I can give is that this discipline stage only lasts a season. It too will pass.

Phase Two: Parents are Personal Trainers (Ages Five to Twelve)

At this stage, a parent is training their children biblically, morally, ethically, and socially. This is where we must be more focused than ever. Here is an easy way to remember our job description at this stage:

Teach them / Tell them / Show them

These three methods of training don't need to be viewed as difficult or overwhelming. We train most effectively by our daily lifestyle. We must develop the mindset that all our actions and words are important.

Children learn most effectively by what they see and hear. We train them by our actions and the words we speak. It matters how we treat our spouse. It matters how we talk about authority figures such as their teachers, coaches, church leaders, or the president. We teach them by our faithfulness to church, and by the level of our generosity. We teach them by the tone in which we speak, and by the atmosphere we set in our homes.

This is the stage that a child will begin to copy, imitate, and reflect their home environment. Our home should be an atmosphere of love, acceptance, openness, forgiveness, and honesty. As we set the pace for our children to follow us, envision them at the age of eighteen and graduating from high school. At that time, what do we want them to be like? That mental picture needs to become our parental goal as we help them reach that destination.

Two of the biggest questions I'm often asked are, "What does training look like?" and, "How do I find time to do it?" Years ago, someone shared an idea with me that helped tremendously. It's called "The Power of Five." These are short, five-minute segments of time focused on one child at a time. It's asking questions such as, "How are you doing? How can I help you? What do you need from me? Tell me about your day." It's telling them how much you love them. A short amount of one-on-one focused time has enormous benefits.

These short moments improve our relationship with our kids. We get a better understanding of their thoughts, problems, gifts, and how we can help improve their personal performance in various areas.

Up to this point, we have been their primary teacher, teaching them right from wrong. At this age, they start attending school. They begin to see the broad range of how other kids act and interact with peers and authority figures. This may be completely different from what we have taught them. It's important for parents to be aware of the negative influences kids will be confronted with, and talk to them about how to interact in the world while maintaining godly values.

One of our greatest resources is being part of a church family. It adds another level and dimension of biblical and social training to our repertoire. For instance, our church's children's ministry goal for its workers is: "Be the greatest friend and best support a parent has ever had."

I love that concept!

Every parent desires any positive support available. That's the benefit and power of the church. The church family provides community for our children. They pray for our kids, encourage them, teach biblical principles, and help develop personal gifts.

The other huge asset the church offers is the Christian lifestyle modeled by children's ministry leaders, youth leaders and other significant adults. These influences are invaluable, and offer great assistance in this important stage of our children.

Kay and I will forever be grateful to our church and the huge investment all the children's and student ministries staff and volunteers invested into our kids. I'm not sure how families raise children effectively without the support of the church.

Parents, let me encourage you that this is not the stage of life to get too busy or lazy with church involvement. I'm not talking about attendance. I'm talking about making the church a focal point for your family life. When you're my age looking back, I can promise that you will view the church as your greatest friend.

Phase Three: Parents are Counselors and Coaches (Ages Twelve to Eighteen)

Too many parents reach this stage and realize they have a rebellious teen on their hands. This primarily happens because they did not understand the importance of proper time investment and discipline.

It's very difficult to discipline and correct bad behavior that should have been a major part of their development in the training stage. This is when parents can enter a war zone, and this can become one of the most unpleasant and painful periods of life.

The day comes for every parent when he or she no longer is the driving influence in their child's life. This can be a difficult time for parents who are extremely close or protective, and they may begin to experience a separation between themselves and their child.

I remember when Kay and I experienced this. My feelings were hurt when one of my sons sought advice from someone other than me, or started hanging out with friends instead of spending time with me. That was painful. I wasn't ready for that separation, but the task of a parent is to encourage a child's growth from dependence to independence.

Too many of us try to continue parenting our teenagers the same way we parented them when they were young. However, teenagers are a different breed. They are like wild stallions, eager to run. Parents often pull hard on the reins as though it's wrong for them to seek independence. In fact, we should encourage that drive for independence and channel it in the right direction.

This is the age for children to develop good decision-making skills. We must give them freedom to make decisions, but also help them understand the consequences of poor decisions. Instead of making decisions for them, ask them what they think. Ask them, "How late do you think you should stay out tonight? Do you think that's the right group of friends to hang out with?" Parents, you will determine quickly if your kids are capable of making good choices.

Remember at this stage, you're a counselor and coach. You're simply calculating how much freedom they can handle. This is not the time to let them run completely free or wild with their own decision making. You're giving them a voice in each situation, which will reveal much about their maturity or immaturity. Slowly and carefully, let them experience making decisions on their own. It's healthy and important for them to start developing these skills.

Teenager should not be allowed to simply tell their parents what they are going to do. For instance, I hear parents say things like, "I just can't get my sixteen-year-old to church. He refuses to come." Or I hear parents say, "I can't choose his friends for him." Or, "I just believe I should respect my teenager's privacy, and I would never go through their phone and read their texts." Parents who believe that have lost sight of their responsibility. At this stage, parents cannot be friends, buddies, or pushovers. We are there to protect from every danger that seeks to destroy the rest of their lives.

Invade their privacy, go through their backpack, look through their phone conversations, put a tracking device on their phone. It is vital to know their location at all times. It goes without saying that children have enormous value. Protect them at all costs, and they will thank you later in life. You are their hope for a great future.

Phase Four: Parents are Consultants (Ages Eighteen and Older)

The most painful season of parenting was the day Kay and I dropped our kids off at college and drove away. Our emotions were all over the place. We were not ready for the separation because we knew from that day forward, life would never be the same. Dropping them off at a dorm room can be frightening on so many levels. But it's less frightening if the parent has successfully navigated the first three phases. Each phase has its own challenges, but phase four can be the most difficult because it requires letting go.

For nearly two decades, you have been your child's commander, personal trainer, counselor and coach. Trying to prolong any of those roles will invite resistance and, perhaps, even resentment.

It is important to realize that even though the separation can be painful, it can also become the most joyful and rewarding stage as you watch your children grow into adulthood. There is no greater reward in all the world than watching them succeed in their career, get married, and have children. And there is such joy in having them become your best friends!

Reflect on Your Childhood

This is one of the most beneficial things you can do as a parent. Reflect on how your parents raised you. How did they interact with you? Were they harsh, impatient, or never around? Were they loving, kind, and consistent? As a child, what did you need from your parents? What went well, and what went wrong?

> *What did your parents do that affected you
> positively or negatively?*

Remember the pain or the joy you experienced as a child. Every day ask yourself the question, "Am I giving my kids the love, attention, and time they need, just as much as I desired it as a child?" If you grew up in a dysfunctional home and did not have a good parental role model, don't let that become an excuse to for you to pass dysfunction down to your kids.

If you didn't have a good role model to follow, watch and learn from parents you know and admire. Nobody is perfect, but there are positive pieces we can pull from those around us. If there's someone you admire as a parent, talk to them. Ask them questions.

Most importantly, never forget what it was like being a kid. This will help us parent with more patience and understanding, allowing us to put ourselves in their shoes, and remembering what we desired and needed when we were children. Then give that to your kids.

When our kids were in elementary school, they would walk home from school. It was a short walk, but it made me nervous due to the length of time it would take for them to get home. I thought, "Why are they taking so long?"

One afternoon I decided I would follow them home at a distance so they wouldn't notice me. I had failed to consider, though, that kids live in a different world than adults.

They stopped to watch a fascinating trail of ants to see where they were going. They made an "educational" stop to watch a man trim large branches out of a tree. They swung around a half dozen telephone poles, and got acquainted with a cute little dog.

I realized I had forgotten what it was like to be eight years old. My kids lived in a completely different world than I did. And I never want to forget that. Reflecting on what I did as a child helps me to be a little more patient, a little more kind, and a little more loving.

Develop Specific Character Traits in Your Children

Identify the characteristics you want your children to have. Some of these might be spiritual strength, biblical wisdom, leadership, confidence, responsibility, kindness, love, or treating everyone the same no matter their status. Those traits will not develop by themselves.

> *As parents, you must be intentional in teaching your children ethically, morally, and spiritually.*

Occasionally, I'll hear a so-called liberated parent say, "I don't want to tilt my child toward any particular religion. I want them to be free to examine the evidence and make up their own mind."

Such comments remind me of a story in the book *You've Got to be Kidding! Real-life Parenting Advice from a Mom and Dad of Nineteen*, by Pat and Ruth Williams:

> A story is told about a conversation between poet Samuel Taylor Coleridge and a man who believed that children should be allowed to do whatever they wanted to do whenever they wanted to do it. "I believe children should be given free rein to think and act," he said, "and thus learn at an early age to make their own decisions. This is the only way they can grow into their full potential." In reply Coleridge said simply, "Come see my flower garden." His visitor followed Coleridge to the back of the house, where he was surprised by the sight of an untidy piece of ground without a single flower in it. "Why, this is nothing but a yard full of weeds," he said. "It used to be filled with roses," Coleridge explained. "But this year I thought I'd

let the garden grow as it willed without tending
to it. This is the result."

If we as parents don't plant faith in God in our children's hearts, we can be assured the weeds will take over. The law of the harvest requires plowing, planting, watering, cultivating, and gathering. Only the fields that are tended to and cared for will produce good fruit.

Unplug from Your Adult World

Think about spending time with your kids like you would think about going on a date. It would be incredibly rude to spend the entire evening looking at your phone while on a date. That is no way to win someone's affection. If you are interested in someone, you will give them your undivided attention. If you don't, you could lose a valuable opportunity.

Last week I was at a playground with our two young granddaughters. There were four young parents with their kids there too. It was interesting to me that the entire time these parents were at the park with their kids, they were also on their phones.

I watched as these parents seemingly were unable to put their phones down long enough to give their children their undivided attention. This might be accepted as normal behavior, but it's harmful. It never crossed those parents' minds that the phone is a tool of distraction and lost moments.

As a grandparent, I desperately wanted to tell those parents not to waste this amazing moment because this "playground" stage will soon be gone forever. At my age, I find myself looking back, wanting more of those undistracted moments with my kids.

Create small, meaningful moments of time when you say to your kids, "I'm turning my phone off so I can just be with you." Watch what happens when you do that. They will light up because there is no one else they would rather be with. You are their hero!

No matter how busy life gets, make sure you are still taking time to connect with each of your kids. Stop long enough to look into their eyes, and let them know they have your undivided attention. Take time to focus on what's important to them.

> *We all love our kids in our hearts, but we must love our kids in our schedule.*

Letter from a Child

Imagine that you're a parent, and you're given a letter like this one.

Dear Mom and Dad,
I remember the best times of my life as those times spent with you. Every memory I have with you is one of the best parts of my life. I will never be little again, or be able to snuggle with you. But my memories bring me comfort and peace when I feel anxious or overwhelmed by the things of life. I often wish I

could be little again! I wish I could spend more time with you, listening to your wisdom, and experiencing the calm, soothing love you gave me. You made my life amazing!

What a great reminder of how important each day is. How will your kids look back and remember you?

Be Intentional with Your Schedule

"Lost time is never found again." Benjamin Franklin wrote these words in *Poor Richard's Almanack* in 1747, and they are a strong reminder to us that time does not stand still. What we do with our time is important, especially regarding our family. Remember to cherish every moment, because children grow up quickly.

As a parent, it can be hard to get out of "parent mode" and simply hang out with our children, but nothing works better than time to builds bonds of laughter and fun. Be intentional and have fun!

In *Fruits of Solitude*, published in The Harvard Classics in 1909-14, William Penn wrote, "Time is what we want the most but…what we use the worst." How true these words are, especially considering our schedule and our children. Let's choose to not only *want* great moments with our children, but to intentionally *create* them.

Remember the day I came home from golfing, and my three little boys couldn't get enough of me? As they wrestled for my attention on the couch, I got up, grabbed my golf clubs, and put them in a closet in our garage. That day I made an intentional decision that nothing, not golf or anything else, would rob my time with my kids.

Those clubs stayed in that closet for the next ten years, and I've never had one day of regret. After that, our Saturdays were filled with playing at the park, hiking in the foothills, going to sports practices, or watching games. That one, small, intentional decision paid huge dividends in my relationship with my kids.

> *Being intentional is simply making small adjustments that produce major improvements.*

Parenting is only a short season of our lives. Don't let anything rob you of that time. When spending time with your kids, don't simply think in terms of large chunks of time. While large family events like a camping trip, a Disney Vacation, or a trip to the beach are important, a bigger impact can be made by centering on frequent, small deposits of time.

For instance, get an ice cream cone on the way home from school, go to the park to play catch, read a story, cuddle on the couch while watching a favorite movie, or pray every night before bedtime. I love remembering the giggles over breakfast, the conversations in the car, and answering "why" for the thousandth time.

Moments matter. The calendar keeps turning. Days go slowly and years go quickly. As parents, the last thing we should do is live with regret of what we didn't do. The safeguard against such regrets is to live in the present.

When our son, Brandon, was a baby, I loved going into his bedroom every morning. As I walked over to the crib, he would get so excited. His big eyes sparkled, and his smile was huge. He'd start jumping up and down. As I picked him up, he'd give me a full body hug with his arms and legs, and then a big kiss. Why was he so excited? He was happy for the dawning of a new day and the opportunity to be with the people he loved.

We should have the same excitement about each day. Each day is another opportunity to love and be loved. We should never forget how to celebrate each day. But as we get older, we can let the challenges of life discourage us and rob us of our happiness. We must realize every day is a gift from God. Once today is gone, we'll never retrieve it.

Don't make the mistake of filling your day with negativity, discouragement, anger, or a sour attitude. Don't waste time thinking you're not appreciated, or nobody likes you. That is a wasted day. Remember, what affects you will affect everybody around you.

Parents, protect your home. Don't squander your days and years by having the wrong mindset. I've made up my mind not to waste any more days. I'm celebrating each day, each of my children, and my spouse as gifts from God! Be intentional with every day that has been given to you.

Survival Mode: The Killer of Intentionality

The number one killer of intentionality in the home is falling into the trap called, "survival mode." If you have small children, you know what that means. This is the season of life when parents might feel completely overwhelmed. At this stage, most of us fight the feelings of guilt that we are failing as a parent.

Kay and I remember that phase of our life vividly. Our three rambunctious boys wanted to participate in every sport that had been invented. The day would start by getting them out of bed, which was a huge challenge in itself. We'd make big lunches: two sandwiches for each boy!

We'd fix breakfast, or make a quick run to a drive-thru. If the boys were eating at home, we'd run through the house gathering backpacks, and their scattered, often unfinished, homework papers off the kitchen table. Then came the shuttle run to different schools. By this time, frustrations were running high from our constant nagging. "Stop watching TV." "Stop just standing there." "Brush your teeth." "Where are your shoes?" "Comb your hair!" "How long are you going to comb your hair?"

After dropping them off at school and coming back into the house, the sight was overwhelming! Beds were unmade, the laundry was piled high on the couch, dishes were in the sink, bedrooms were a wreck, and the day barely begun.

It's called "survival mode," and the ultimate goal of each day was simply to make it to the end of the day with as little drama as possible. But, surviving another day is a discouraging way to live. It's miserable for everyone because there's no plan, organization, clear goal, or purpose. If we are not intentional on guiding our children toward a preferred lifestyle, then there is a world waiting to teach them what is deemed important.

Family Dinners

One memory that stands out in our family is joining around the dinner table. Both Kay and I believed that gathering the family for meal time was important. But we didn't think through the next step on why it's important.

We would gather for dinner, and because it was one of the few times all of us were together, the conversation naturally gravitated to confronting problems, attitudes, grades, or an array of issues. At times, tempers would flare and bad attitudes would manifest themselves. We would argue over why grades were low.

I remember one evening at the dinner table, Kay and I were extremely frustrated over one of the boy's low grades. In his opinion, it was the teacher's fault. We firmly set the record straight, "It's not the teacher's fault, it's yours!" The tension kept building and building until he burst into tears, jumped up from the table knocking over his chair, and ran to his room yelling, "You're being so unfair to me." The bedroom door slammed!

There was a long, awkward silence at the table. In fact, it was very uncomfortable. After the other two boys were excused from the table I remember saying to Kay, "I will never let that happen again at dinner." That was the day we became intentional about the importance of the dinner table.

Kay became a master at intentional scheduling. She scheduled our weekly dinners on Tuesdays, Wednesdays, and Thursdays, immediately following our boys' football or baseball practices. Everyone knew that dinner attendance was mandatory. We made a rule that the table was a family gathering, a place for fun, laughter, stories, encouragement, listening, and talking about our day.

Discipline and correction would have its place in our family, but it would not take place at the dinner table. We guarded this as a sacred time of bonding, so everyone would look forward to it, and not dread it. Throughout the high school years, there were many times we sat at the table telling stories and laughing until our sides hurt.

Other times, someone would open up about a deep hurt or disappointment they were experiencing. As the tears flowed, it became a time of consoling, and with all of us sitting around the table together, it brought needed comfort.

It was such a meaningful time that our boys would often bring friends to join us. Many of them were from broken homes and had never experienced a family interaction like that. This also benefitted Kay and I as we became connected to their friends and their social world.

That small, intentional decision changed the dynamics of our home almost more than anything else. In fact, even though our three boys are now grown, and married, and have their own children, every Monday night, all seventeen of us gather around the dinner table where Kay has prepared an amazing home-cooked meal. We tell stories of our week, laughing and enjoying each other's company.

> *The greatest gift in life is a tightly-woven family.*

Families need to have fun together and enjoy themselves. As parents, our role is to help our family laugh, be crazy, have fun, and be adventurous. Children need these memories to create a sense of stability and security, which will provide a vital foundation for them in becoming healthy adults.

Ask yourself, "What fun thing have I done with my family lately?" If you can't think of an answer, then be creative, plan a meaningful activity, and have some fun!

CHAPTER 5

Foundation 3 – Discipline

A n old saying states, "Discipline is the difference between what you want now and what you want most." We can say something similar about parenting.

> *Your job as a parent is to make your kids do what they don't want to do, so they can become who God created them to be.*

Parents, your greatest contribution in life may not be what you do, but who you raise.

Discipline has a twofold definition: 1) to punish or penalize for the sake of enforcing obedience and perfecting moral character; and 2) the practice of training children to obey rules or a code of behavior. Look carefully again at this definition. The first definition's key word is punish. The second definition's key word is train.

As parents of young children, when we hear the word discipline, we immediately think of things like a swatting them on the butt, placing them in time out, demanding an apology, or sending them to their room. There is absolutely a need for all those things, but when we think proactively about discipline, we can keep from having to do it so often. As our children grow, our goal is to focus less on discipline, and focus more on investing time to hone skills they can use throughout their lives. By proactively training our kids, we won't have to retrain bad habits or wrong thinking as they approach adulthood.

Teach Them to Do Chores

Proactive discipline is teaching kids to do chores, such as picking up toys, taking out the garbage, making a bed, cleaning a room, mowing the lawn, or doing dishes. These are not simply ways to make a parent's life easier, they're ways to make a child's life better too. When children do chores, they realize, "I have to do the work of life in order to be part of life."

Think about how damaging it is for kids who grow into teens but don't know how to make their beds properly, clean their room, wash dishes, do laundry, or help with yard work. These are basic skills every teenager needs to know. How they do life as a teenager will carry over into their adult world. If they never learned to have a good work ethic, that can create havoc when they are married.

Simply turning twenty-one or getting married doesn't mean someone can flip a switch and become instantly mature. Everyone will carry the habits they formed as a child. If these simple tasks are missing in a teenager's life, the correction needs to start quickly to help them be prepared for the life that's right in front of them.

> *Work is also a great form of discipline. It has an amazing power to correct a bad attitude, a smart mouth, or a foolish action.*

When our kids were teenagers, we were landscaping our backyard. One day, I had a huge pile of rock delivered to the house. We were hauling it in a wheelbarrow from the front yard to the backyard. We had a saying during that time if one of the boys got in trouble. I'd say, "I'm sending you to the rock pile." We still laugh about that. It's amazing how manual labor can straighten out wrong behavior. I'm a big believer that work is a very effective form of discipline. I'm not a fan of sending kids to their rooms to do nothing. I'm a fan of them working and doing something productive.

Teach Them Social Skills

Have you ever worked with socially-awkward people? It will probably be no surprise to learn that multiple studies at several universities have found that kids with good social skills are successful in life.

Children who are more helpful to others, more empathetic, and able to resolve problems on their own will more likely earn a college degree and have a full-time job by age twenty-five, than those who had limited social skills. There is no shortage of teenagers I have talked with that give one-word responses. Sometimes, they might simply shrug their shoulders. Other times, they barely open their mouth to mumble something unintelligible. Kids should not settle into those kinds of habits. Instead, teach kids the proper way to start a conversation, get someone's attention, or join a group of kids already playing together.

Many children do not know how to handle interpersonal social situations that involve following directions, holding a proper conversation, listening, giving compliments, or developing proper behavior during times of teasing or bullying. These are all situations that can be discussed at the dinner table or in the car on the way to school.

Our middle son, Jonathan, was somewhat shy, and at the age of thirteen, did not communicate with adults very well. He had a weak handshake, very little to say, and little confidence. As parents, we must be the ones to take the initiative to develop their social skills. Don't ignore it, develop it. I began having Jonathan stand with me at the front door of our church every Sunday morning. Together, we shook hands and visited with everyone walking out the doors. I instructed him to greet people with a firm and confident hand shake, and look directly in their eyes. I encouraged him to ask questions about their lives. In a very short amount of time, he became a good communicator, and easily engages in adult conversations.

The value Jonathan found in developing these skills was fully realized when he sat in front of the board of pharmacy, interviewing to be accepted into the university's school of pharmacy. Today as a pharmacist, the main part of his job is communicating, instructing, and counseling people on their medications and medical conditions.

One small, training exercise on how to interact with people greatly enhanced his abilities and was one of the catalysts of him becoming a Doctor of Pharmacy.

Teach Them Financial Responsibility

When I was twelve years old, I landed my first big job. I was working for the Amarillo Tribune newspaper company. The glorious position I held: Paper Boy.

Every day I came home after school, the newspaper company had delivered a big stack of newspapers in our driveway. I would haul them into the house, roll up each one, and neatly place it in the big canvas bag they had provided. I placed the bag over the handle bars of my bicycle, and began delivering newspapers. Every month, I had to go door-to-door collecting payment from all my costumers. Everyone paid in cash, and I would come home with a bag full of one-dollar bills. Spreading the cash out on my bed, I thought I was a millionaire.

The first thing I did was to take out the amount I owed the newspaper company and push it to one side. Then I would count out 10 percent of my money and push it to the opposite side—that belonged to God. The rest of the money was mine to use however I wanted.

As I look back on that, the odd thing is, I never remember my mom or dad specifically teaching me about the principle of tithing. Yet, I did it without any hesitation, and I've been a strong financial supporter of the church all my life. Where did that come from? Why is that such a part of my life?

It was displayed to me by my parents on a weekly basis. We had a family ritual in which mom would bake two pies every Saturday night. These were the best pies in the world. We would all gather around the television and watch the weekly episode of *Gunsmoke*. Just as it was starting, mom would ask each one of us which pie we wanted. I always did what my dad did. He would say, "I'll take a little of both," and I would also have a little of both. Great memories!

More importantly, I remember something else about those Saturday nights. At some point, one of my parents would write out a check for tithes, and place it by their Bible to take to church the next morning. It was a pattern of great consistency. It was a part of their life. Tithing was as normal as eating and breathing. It was as much of a routine as eating pie on Saturday night. The thought of not doing it was ridiculous. Their way of life became my way of life, and what they did, I still do to this day.

> *Parents, the greatest injustice you will ever do to your children is not teach them to tithe their income to the house of God.*

When a Christian family chooses to be disobedient with their finances, they are deliberately choosing to disregard the instruction God gave us.

Maybe you don't believe the New Testament teaches tithing. While it's true that it doesn't use that word specifically, it applies an even more strict command of generosity for born-again believers. The New Testament teaches that believers share in the Spirit of Christ, which is expressed through radical love and generosity. As New Testament believers, we do not give out of obligation, but out of love and gratitude for the gift of eternal life given to us. Our giving is the gateway for others to find that same gift of eternal life.

Statistics reveal that 87 percent of church-attending parents do not tithe. Thus, we are training our children to disregard one of the clearest and most important spiritual mandates in the Bible. Vision cannot move forward without every believer making a sacrificing. Think about this: the church, which is the very institution that feeds us and our children spiritually, can struggle if we refuse to care for it with our finances.

Tithing is the first and most important financial discipline which will prepare our children for future success. Here are questions every Christian parent must ask themselves:

- Do I want my kids to grow into adulthood as tithers or non-tithers?
- Am I raising my children to be self-consumed or focused on God?
- Am I raising kids to follow God's commands or to live by their own set of rules?

When it comes to God and money, the key point is trust. Do you trust God or yourself? Do you give to His work having complete faith and trust that He will provide for all your needs? It is not about the amount of money that we have; it is about the amount of trust in God that we have!

For some reason, most parents do a poor job on educating their kids on financial responsibility. Take every opportunity to teach your kids about the power of money and how to control it, instead of becoming a slave to it. Once they have left home, too many young adults find themselves buried with student loans, credit card debt, and car loans. They have become slaves to the lenders. We can never start too early explaining to our kids why so many people get into debt. Debt brings undue stress into their lives, simply because they spend more than they make.

This sounds elementary, but most people don't even take the time to track their income and expenses. Teaching our kids simple ways to budget their allowance, track their expenses, and stay within their limits will set them up for success.

Before our kids leave home, here are some financial conversations to have with them:

- teach them contentment
- teach them the principle of tithing
- give them the responsibility of a bank account
- show them how to save for college
- teach them to avoid student loans if possible
- teach them the danger of credit cards
- show them how a budget works
- introduce them to the magic of compound interest
- teach them about retirement planning

Teaching and training about money is proactive training. It's a discipline that must be in place before they leave home. Many parents struggle in this area of finances and feel very inept to teach their own children. Let me encourage you to take advantage of great teaching tools such as *Financial Peace University* by Dave Ramsey. This course is an absolute must for every high school or college-age student. The information and wisdom they will receive from this course will advance them financially years beyond their peers. Financial freedom brings tremendous peace into our lives.

Teach and Demonstrate High Educational Expectations

Midway through a school year, some students may have disappointing grades, but they may be reluctant to take ownership of their performance. Some teens are not emotionally mature enough for the independence they so desperately want. They struggle to take responsibility for their poor grades, or blame their failure on the teachers. It's also hard for kids to see the big picture. They live in the present, and see no benefits from studying subjects such as math or history. The challenge for us is to teach them academic responsibility.

Learning is Valuable

The value of school comes from the parent. If your kids know you value it, they will begin to understand the importance of taking ownership of their studies. Parents should be aware of the school's academic expectations, monitor their kids' homework assignments, and make sure kids have a study space in the house. This is not laying on their bed or in front of the television.

You may need to step in and take control if you see these warning signs appear: poor organizational and time-management skills, falling grades, missing assignments, or displays of anger and frustration. These are signs a student may be struggling and desperately needs a parent to step in and help get them back on track.

If this happens, it's important that parents explain to their kids not to pass blame to anybody else. Teach them to take responsibility, and work with them on how to communicate with a teacher. Be careful not to control them but give strong guidance.

Motivate Them

If a child is struggling with their grades, don't simply focus on their grades, but start praising them for the effort they are making. Learning a strong work ethic is more important for long-term growth. Throughout life, we might struggle in different areas, but hard work and determination can allow us to overcome these difficulties. It's vital to instill and build up a sense of hard work and determination in a child.

Academic success produces major benefits in our kids. Studies show they will have higher self-esteem, lower levels of depression and anxiety, be more socially-inclined, and be less likely to abuse alcohol or illegal substances. Positive self-esteem and self-confidence are critical factors for their futures.

Being academically disciplined is not only good for their future, it's also good while they are still at home. Kids coming home with bad grades places significant stresses on a family, and produces high levels of family tension. Creating proactive academic discipline brings a tremendous amount of peace into the home.

Getting to the Heart of Your Child's Behavior

Discipline is one of the biggest challenges we face as parents. Too many parents focus on changing a child's behavior by a disciplinary action and stopping there. Wrong behavior must be corrected, but the more important issue is to understand what is happening in the child's heart.

The Bible teaches that the heart is the control center for life. A person's life reflects his heart. Proverbs 4:23 states, "Above all else, guard your heart, for everything you do flows from it." The word picture here is of a wellspring. In other words, the heart is a well from which all the issues of life flow out. The behavior a person exhibits is an expression of the overflow of the heart. The heart determines behavior. What a person says and does expresses the orientation of their heart.

Luke 6:45 states, "A good man brings good things out of the good stored up in his heart, and an evil man brings evil things out of the evil stored up in his heart." These scriptures are imperative for the task of parenting. They teach us that behavior is not the real issue, the heart is the issue. Parents often get sidetracked with behavior, because it's what they see. Behavior irritates and frustrates, and can become the focus of discipline. What is the real problem? Behavior, whether good or bad, comes from somewhere. It reflects what's deep down inside a person. What should concern us more than the behavior is the attitudes of the heart that drive the behavior.

Jesus addresses this heart issue with the Pharisees in Matthew 15, denouncing those who have honored him with their lips but not their hearts. Jesus compared these people to those who continually wash the outside of a cup while neglecting to wash the inside. This is what we often do in parenting. We demand changed behavior without addressing the heart that drives the behavior. We want to wash the outside of the cup that everybody sees while ignoring the inside that nobody sees.

Let me use an example that is very familiar to anyone who has two or more children. The children are playing, and a fight breaks out over a toy. The classic parent response is, "Who had it first?" However, this response misses heart issues. "Who had it first?" is an issue of justice. Justice operates in the favor of the child who was quicker in getting the toy. Therefore, children learn that whoever sees, grabs, or controls the toy first is the winner.

However, if we look at this situation in terms of the heart, the situation changes. Now, there are two offenders. Both children are displaying a hardness of heart toward the other. Both are being selfish. Both children are saying, "I don't care about you or your happiness. I am only concerned about myself. I want this toy. My happiness depends on possessing it. I will have it regardless of what you want." Two children are preferring themselves over the other. One has the toy and is keeping the advantage. The other is jealous and wants what they have. Both children are displaying a heart issue, "I want my happiness, even at your expense." Even though it's not easy, we must address behavior, but we can't stop there. We must address the attitude of the heart.

Put the Ball of Responsibility in Their Court

Here is a strategy that never has to change. If you've asked your child to do something, and they have not done it, they don't get to go to the next fun event, no matter what that event is.

For example, you ask your son to clean his room, but two hours later, it's clearly not done. If your child is eight, he might be expecting to go buy a football you promised him. If your child is sixteen, she might want to go to a movie with friends. In either case, simply say, "You're not going." Then, turn and walk away. If your child follows you, don't announce your strategy. It works better if your child figures out the situation for himself. He will quickly put two and two together. His action of disobedience results in the next enjoyable activity being removed from him. This only works if you are fully committed and consistent in your discipline strategy.

Understand that when you start applying these techniques, the attitudes and behaviors of your children may get worse for a time. Don't panic; it means you're on the right track. The most important thing is that remain consistent. Keep the ball of responsibility in their court, not yours. With this method, there is no harassing, threatening, powerless warnings, or counting to three. This helps tremendously in eliminating wars with your kids. It's not foolproof or the "fix-all," but it absolutely improves your child's obedience over a period of time.

Your children will pick up in a hurry when this reaction to their disobedience is normal. They will also quickly learn that the ball is in their court. They decide if they want to enjoy or forfeit the next fun activity. After they miss a few, they will think twice before ignoring their responsibility. I love that this leaves the decision-making in their hands, and makes them think about rewards and consequences of obedience and disobedience.

A Strong-Willed Child (SWC)

Let me address discipline at a more challenging level. What do you do as a parent when you become completely overwhelmed by what you would describe as a strong-willed child (SWC)?

Every parent knows the feeling: your child just drew on the wall with a permanent marker, or mouthed off to you for what feels like the millionth time. They defiantly tell you, "No," and you're at your wit's end.

For some children, these moments of defiance are simply moments. But, for strong-willed children, these "moments" are a way of life, which can test the resolve of even the most patient parent. When you find yourself in this situation, it's easy to focus on who or what is to blame rather than on what can be done to improve the situation. We may even wonder if it can be improved.

We see character traits, actions, and attitudes that concern us. Our mind runs wild with the fear of what our child's future will look like. Is my non-compliant child doomed to become a challenging adolescent? Will he or she become a defiant teenager, refusing to comply with requests and completely rebelling? Will my child have any chance of growing into adulthood and find God's purpose for their life, or will they self-destruct?

If any of this sounds familiar, take heart, as we all experience these feelings at different times. Fortunately, defiance is not a permanent trait but a behavior that can be changed through positive interactions. We know from science and research that strong-willed children are often world changers. They're natural-born leaders, who typically pave the way when no one else will. Strong-willed kids are not going to let the world change them. They will change the world.

That's something to admire. An SWC can think independently and stand firm for what he or she believes. If you look at adults who are successful, they are the people who won't let obstacles keep them from their goals. They see a challenge and meet it head-on. They are determined and committed people who can make a real difference in the world. If you have an SWC, you are basically parenting a child who will become a world-changer. It's a heavy burden to carry. The stakes are high, because one day they will be a leader. The question becomes, "Will their influence be positive or negative upon society and those they lead?"

Give Your Child Opportunities for Leadership

Stop looking at your child as a problem child and view them as a leader or a world-changer. If their natural bent is to crave power and control, feed their extraordinary need of overseeing something instead of starving their need.

Our grandson, Asher, can be labeled an SWC. He has an overwhelming need to be in control and to lead. I have never seen this level of intensity in any other child I've met.

He's playing football this year and he likes it, but he would enjoy the sport far more if he could be the coach or referee. One day, he was trying to take a whistle and a megaphone with him to practice. He believed these two things would give him power to take control of the team. Had he made it out of the car with those things, it would have been the best day of his life. At his young age, he truly believes his way is not just the right way, but the only way.

One time in his elementary school, they had an active shooter drill. The teacher explained this very difficult and important drill, and what the steps of action the class would take if they had an intruder. In the process, she had everyone huddle in the corner of the room. Asher did not huddle with them. She called his name to join them, and his response was, "This is a really bad plan. I don't know who came up with this, but it's wrong. I'm not going to huddle in a corner for someone to come in here and shoot us. Here is my plan..." Obviously, that didn't go over very well with the teacher, and his mom and dad were called in for a parent-teacher conference over the power struggle of whose plan would work best. That's an SWC that has a need to be in control. While our world needs these leaders, the problem is maintaining sanity while raising them!

By school-age, let a strong-willed child help put together a work schedule for household chores, helping choose who's responsible for what. Put them in charge of drawing up a calendar and posting it on the wall. Help them find a cause, such as volunteering in the kid's area at church, where they can oversee something. Help them do kind things for an elderly neighbor. Appoint them as the leader of the next family activity or outing. Find out what interests them and push them into athletics, academics, or musical endeavors that will develop their personal fortitude. If your SWC has a bent for control and power, gently guide it and feed it, instead of constantly battling with them.

If you teach an SWC to do what is right, they will do what is right with a strong will. That's what the world needs!

Ease Your Child's Strong Will with Tenderness and Love

It's easy to become so tired and frustrated with a strong-willed child, that we can forget to be tender, gentle, and loving. Yet without our example, our children cannot learn to be tender and gentle themselves.

Find routine times each day to physically touch and hug your children, and talk to them in a tender, loving voice. If a child is acting up or losing control, this is the exact moment he or she needs a parent the most. He or she needs guidance, teaching, coaching, and a parent who doesn't lose control. Understand that inside an SWC's heart and mind are swirling emotions, like a tilt-o-whirl at the state fair. Their emotions may be spinning without logic. Instead of ignoring the behavior, sending kids to their rooms, or escalating emotionally, draw closer to children. Don't turn away from them.

More than anything, strong-willed children want a parent who will recognize their side of the story. Start taking notice when they lose control, because most often it will be when they feel they have no voice, or don't have the opportunity to be heard. This method can be difficult and time consuming, but it can reduce explosive moments in the long run. There is no need to change any boundaries, but they need time to explain their viewpoint.

Try using open-ended statements like these:

- You don't want to _____.
- You don't like that because_____.
- You wish you could _____ instead.

Use these probing statements without sarcasm or frustration. Speak with sincere empathy. Take time to look them in their eyes. It validates them, and works better than ignoring, or abruptly saying, "No," to their somewhat illogical thought-process.

They are processing why and when they need something, and they need you to process with them.

What Impact Does an SWC Have on His or Her Family?

The presence of an SWC in a family can drive a wedge not only between you and your child, but also between you and your spouse. I've been in the ministry for many years, and had hundreds of conversations with parents seeking help and advice. I've had competent Christian parents say to me with deep sadness, "You know what? I think I dislike or even hate my child. I hate to say it, but that's how I feel."

It's easy for parents to become so irritated and worn out by their kids' negative behavior, that it removes all enjoyment of family life, and they can forget the good that is in their child.

If you find yourself at this point, your tendency will be to isolate from them. Fight against that destructive impulse. Take advantage of every opportunity to spend short amounts of time with your SWC. Go to the store together, run a quick errand, go to the car wash, or have them sit next to you on the couch and snuggle with them. Take them to get ice cream or a lemonade, telling them, "This is just because I love you so much." In these quick, short moments, avoid confrontation. There is plenty of time for that, but don't let it happen here. Think of these times as special bonding moments. I like to think of them as "love-burst moments." It's not the fix-all, but it's a gigantic step in the right direction.

It's essential that an SWC knows that they are loved without question, because so much of their life is filled with contention, strife, or being disciplined. I encourage parents to write notes that say, "Here's what I like about you," or, "This is why I love you so much." These can go a long way toward reminding the SWC that despite your battles, you do love them. Preserving the parent-child relationship must come before preserving a sense of order in the house, or getting chores and homework done at a prescribed time.

The priority is working on your relationship with them before focusing on all the rules. You must use common sense here. Think about it this way: if you come home every night to someone who nags and yells and gripes at you, soon you won't want to come home. Instead of home being a refuge, it becomes a place to avoid. For home life to have any chance of being successful, there must be a strong sense of family bonds and love. Relationships are our highest priority and the best investment anyone can make.

Knee-Jerk Discipline

Remember that a constant battle for control is exhausting. As a parent, you will be tempted, through your constant frustration, to increase the frequency or severity of your discipline to show your children who is in charge.

When your child is testing you for power and control, it's easy to default to a standard punishment such as a time-out, loss of a privilege, spanking, or yelling. The problem is yelling and spanking aren't long-term solutions. You might enjoy an immediate result, that is, the child stops an undesired behavior, but in the end, yelling or physical punishment simply continues the cycle of the battle of the wills with very little progress. Instead of resorting to knee-jerk punishments, slow down and think about the most effective discipline. Remember discipline is corrective and restorative.

> *Discipline is fixing what went wrong, so the child can learn from a mistake and not repeat destructive behavior.*

If a child is mean to his or her sister, perhaps he or she should clean the sister's room. This type of discipline helps children process that mean actions must be replaced with kind actions. If children are older, it is in order to have them write a letter of apology to their siblings admitting they're wrong.

A well-known pastor uses this illustration. A teenage son acts extremely disrespectful to his mother one day. When the father hears what happened, he steps in with frustration and anger toward his son, because of how he's treated his mother. The father loses his temper, they have a verbal exchange, and he sends his son to his room. Tempers flare and tensions are high. As the son is going into his room, his father declares he's grounded for a month. The son sits alone in his room brooding and angry, thinking about how much he dislikes his parents. Over the next several days, or perhaps weeks, the tension between him and his parents grows more intense.

However, let's change the scenario. When the father finds out about his son's disrespectful actions toward his mother, he doesn't lose his temper. He sends his son to his room without showing anger or frustration. The father gives himself time to cool down and to think logically about how to deal with this unacceptable behavior. A little later the father walks into his son's room and tells him that kind of behavior can never happen again. He tells his son, "This is what you must do. In a few moments, you're going to apologize to your mother and tell her you are embarrassed by your actions. Then I want you to ask your mother out on a date to a nice restaurant, and pay for it with your own money." Instead of allowing the son to sit in his bedroom, fuming about how mean his parents are, he now has some constructive tasks to accomplish. The son must make a reservation at a restaurant, possibly even mowing a few lawns to raise the money to pay for the meal. He will sit with his mother at the restaurant treating her like a queen. This will be a night spent mending a relationship and possibility creating a special moment they both will never forget.

What a training moment! This is the reason the Bible tells us to be slow to anger. When we are too quick with our response, or have a knee-jerk reaction, we miss a teachable moment that allows both our children and us to grow. The biggest key to discipline is to be careful not to get caught in a heated moment and verbally explode like a volcano, gushing out a flood of disciplinary threats. It's much healthier and wiser to give yourself time to think of the best form of discipline that's not simply a punishment, but most importantly, how it can restore the wrong that has been done.

Affection Balances Discipline

There are numerous studies on the positive effects, both physically and emotionally, of physical touch. Starting in infancy, large amounts of affection create a strong bond between a parent and child. As children get older, be playful by doing fun activities together, like dancing, creating silly games, or pretending to be a hugging or kissing monster.

When my dad came home from work, he would wrestle on the floor with us. When he kissed us on the forehead, it was the moment he declared victory; and he won every time. This is a very silly game, but that is precisely the point. It's silly, playful, and childlike, but it speaks volumes of love to a child!

What I learned from my dad, I carried on to my kids. I reached out to them to touch and acknowledge them often. I walked through the living room and patted them on the back. I ruffled their hair, or gave them a gentle pat with a smile. This is the power of bonding you cannot afford to miss. Sadly, I've observed in many homes that the dog receives more physical attention than the kids.

In a recent *Trolls* movie, the trolls wore watches with alarm clocks that would go off every hour for hug time. If that's what it takes, set an alarm. Make sure to give your kids a hug during certain times of the day, such as before they leave for school, when they get home from school, and before bedtime.

Another important act of affection that can be done after having to discipline your child is to give them a hug at the end of the conversation. Even though they know you are not pleased with their behavior, they know you still love them.

In saying all of that, be careful not to go overboard and smother your kids. Respect their individual comfort level, and be aware that this will change as they go through different stages. Yet, I would put this as one of the highest priorities of parenting. I cannot overemphasize the power of a tender, loving touch.

CHAPTER 6

Foundation 4 – Consistency

When I was a teenager during the summer, I was home when my dad came home for lunch. The exact same scene played out every day. He would rush in and greet me like he hadn't seen me in months, even though I had seen him just a few hours earlier. He would go into the kitchen to make a sandwich. But this was never a whole sandwich. It was half a sandwich. He never dirtied a plate, but would use a piece of wax paper instead. He'd use a paper cup of water. All of this was done in record time. Then he would go into the living room and lay down on the floor saying out loud, "All I need is ten minutes," meaning that all he needed was a ten-minute power nap. Almost instantly he would be breathing heavily, sound asleep. In exactly ten minutes he would jump to his feet, stretch, and say in a loud voice, "Oh, I feel good!" As quickly as he had arrived, he was heading out the door saying, "I'll see you after work!" He said it in such a tone that you would think it was going to be a major event. That scene played out hundreds of times with no variations, and as a kid, I couldn't help but be amused by him. My dad was one of the most consistent people I have ever known.

The very word consistency leaves no wiggle room to live in the in-between. A person is either consistent or they are not. Although consistency is so important, it is one of the most common parenting pitfalls. That's because consistency is not easy. It requires dedication, and learning to be steadfast and steady with emotions, words, and actions even when we feel tired, irritable, and exhausted.

Parental consistency can be defined as doing something the same way from one time to the next. It means that if a child breaks a family rule, it will be dealt with in the same way whenever it happens. It means that the same expectations and reinforcements are clearly followed every day. That makes life predictable.

It is extremely confusing for a child to experience a harsh emotional outburst one moment and kindness the next. Inconsistency in any area of our life will lead us toward failure. The greatest compliment a parent can receive is that they were a picture of healthy consistency. Parenting with consistency does more than improve a child's behavior. It also creates a sense of security which produces a greater level of peace in the home.

Routine and predictability stabilize a home environment. Parents need to be the stabilizing constant in their children's lives. Children are confronted with change daily, which creates stress. In fact, the very definition of growing up is change. Children's bodies are changing daily. Babies and toddlers give up pacifiers, bottles, and cribs. They go from crawling to walking. New teachers and classmates come and go every year. Children acquire new skills and information at an astonishing pace, from reading, to crossing the street, to learning soccer, to riding a bike. Few children live in the same house during their entire childhood. Most will move several times. These moves can be to new cities or new neighborhoods, schools, and churches. Children live in a world of fast-paced change. That's why children love familiar and predictable routines. A parent's role is to help their children navigate through all the new challenges and developmental stages, while at the same time, giving them as much consistent structure as possible.

Structure and routines teach kids how to constructively control themselves and their environments. Have you ever noticed how our kids love certain routines? They want to read the same book, listen to the same song, and watch the same movie repeatedly. I've watched the movies *Cinderella* and *Frozen* so many times with our granddaughters, I can recite every conversation and song verbatim.

> *Consistency is one of the keys to living a blessed life, because it's a disciplined life.*

We chose to be in control of our life, instead of letting life's circumstances control us. Parents that consistently model structure and routine teach their kids how to constructively control themselves and their environments. Kids who come from chaotic homes where they are not held responsible to put their belongings away, or make their beds, or do their homework, or complete certain household responsibilities will never learn how to consistently accomplish unpleasant tasks. The danger is that those habits can follow them the rest of their lives.

> *Help your children develop constructive habits of responsibility. You're helping them develop traits of success for their future.*

Parents who tend to take structure too far can also cause problems. Structure must be imposed with sensitivity. Don't become rigid and legalistic with rules. I've always been a believer that rules should be broken when larger relationship issues are at stake. In other words, you must learn how to parent with flexibility. Structure and routine should not be oppressive. Think of them as friends that makes home life cozier and more peaceful. Over time, your kids will begin to internalize the ability to structure their own lives.

How many people do we run into that are constantly talking about how hard life is? Everything in their lives is bad. They are constantly focused on problems, which produces a constant state of being in a bad mood and frustrated. They are not fun to be around.

Research shows that we think, on average, forty-two thoughts per minute. Over the course of a day, that's about sixty thousand thoughts. What is striking about that, is over forty thousand of those thoughts are negative. Have you noticed how easy and natural it is to gravitate to negativity? We all lean toward it, because we born with a sinful, broken nature.

> *We must renew our mind through biblical principles,*
> *establishing new habits of thinking.*

Thoughts form patterns and habits. But, we have complete control over our minds. A consistently negative person is someone with little discipline over their thoughts.

When I was thirteen-years-old, one night we were out at dinner with friends from church. The husband and wife were constantly bickering with each other while we sat at the table. They seemed to be extremely frustrated and agitated with each other. I can remember how uncomfortable and unpleasant it was, and I couldn't wait for dinner to be over. On the way home from the restaurant, my dad asked me, "Do you know why those people we had dinner with tonight are so miserable?" I said, "No." He said, "Because they choose to be miserable. Galen, always remember this: bickering, arguing, and fighting in marriage is nothing more than a habit you create. Never start it and you'll never have to live in the misery of it."

That made such a huge impression on my life, that I still remember it to this day. In fact, the night I was getting married, I was standing alone in a side room ten minutes before walking onto the stage for the ceremony. I was excited as well as nervous. My mind was racing in a hundred different directions. While I was standing there all those years later, my dad's words came back to me. "Bickering, arguing, and fighting in marriage is nothing more than a habit you create. Never start it and you'll never have to live in the misery of it."

That's one of the hallmarks that I consistently strive for,

because I want to add benefit to the lives of people around me and not add stress and anxiety. Being consistent in kindness and respect toward the people you love the most is the greatest gift you can give them.

Here are five words that describe consistency: constant, steady, reliable, stable, and persistent. These five powerful words explain the power and the need for consistency. It needs to be at the forefront of our personal life that also transfers over into our parenting.

Your Consistency is Your Influence

One of the main reasons my mom and dad had such a huge influence in my life is that they were always consistent. Whether at church, home, or on vacation, whether stressed or happy, whether experiencing disappointments and loss or enjoying successes in life, they were consistent. When they came home from work every day, I never had to wonder who was going to walk through the front door. I knew and looked forward to it!

My dad was a blue-collar laborer working for a gas company. He spent his days climbing on rooftops of buildings or working in alleyways. He would come home tired and dirty, but when he came through that door, it was always a grand entrance! He was happy, glad to be home, and glad to see us. He was light-hearted, silly, funny, affectionate, and kind. As I look back, I realize he gave us his best no matter what type of day he had.

There is no greater gift we could give our families. We must give them our best instead of letting them always see our worst.

We tend to look at negative people and say, "Well, that's just who they are. That's just their personality and temperament." That's not true. It has nothing to do with personality or temperament. It has everything to do with choice. For instance, moodiness is inconsistent behavior. No one ever knows what to expect. Who's going to walk through the door today: Hannibal Lecter or Mother Teresa? The last person I want to spend time with is someone who can't control their emotions. Every moody person will tell you they just can't help being that way. They are mad, or sad, or angry because of what someone said or did, and it set them off.

> *Circumstances are driving their mood and behavior, instead of them choosing their mood and behavior.*

People make false statements when they say they cannot control their emotions or their anger. This is an excuse to say things that are harsh and hurtful. We have far more self-control than we think. For instance, someone might be in an absolute rage, yelling and screaming at their spouse or children, and completely out-of-control. However, if the phone rings at that exact moment and it's a friend, they can instantly go from out-of-control behavior to a calm, controlled voice.

> *It's not that we are unable to control our emotions, words and actions; it's that we are unwilling.*

We must value the power of controlled consistency to bless others with our consistency. It is one of the most admirable traits a person can obtain, and those are the people we respect.

Middle "C"

Max Lucado recounts a wonderful story in his book, *Grace for the Moment, Vol. II,*

> When Lloyd C. Douglas, author of *The Robe* and other novels, was a university student, he lived in a boarding house. Downstairs on the first floor was an elderly, retired music teacher who was homebound and unable to leave the apartment. Douglas said that every morning they had a ritual they would go through together. He would come down the steps, open the old man's door, and ask, "Well, what's the good news?" The old man would pick up his tuning fork; tap it on the side of his wheelchair and say, "That's middle C! It was middle C yesterday; it will be middle C tomorrow; it will be middle C a thousand years from now. The tenor upstairs sings flat, the piano across the hall is out of tune, but, my friend, THAT IS MIDDLE C!"

The old man had discovered one thing upon which he could depend, one constant reality that never changes in a changing world. As parents, we need to be the middle "C" in our kids' lives, that is, the constant reality that never changes.

Consistency in Rules and Consequences

Discipline seems abrupt and unfair to a child if rules and expectations are not clearly defined, established in advance, and reinforced daily. Create a few clear family rules and the consequences for breaking them. Rules should stay consistent no matter the circumstance.

Every parent falls into the trap of threatening too big and not delivering. We all have done this futile exercise: "I'm going to count to three and then you're going to get it. I'm serious! I hope you're listening! Here I go, one, *twooooo*, two and a half, two and three quarters, I don't see you moving. I'm almost at three." Then we say it, "THREE!" And they are still standing there in defiance, and we don't know what else to do but start counting all over again.

Setting and maintaining rules in a family is one of the cardinal rules of good parenting. Don't set a rule unless it is important, and you are willing to enforce it.

One of the habits I fell into early in parenting was saying, "No," before I even thought through why I was saying, "No." I might later realize that wasn't the right answer and then change my answer to say, "Yes." My kids began to figure out that, "No," means I might change my mind. And that's nothing but trouble! If you are not good at holding true to your "No," try saying, "Maybe," or "We'll see." Then you're not deflating the power of your, "No."

Once a rule is set, it's equally important to set the consequence for breaking the rule. If you set a curfew for 10 p.m. on school nights and 11:30 p.m. on weekends, with agreed upon exceptions for special events, then stick with it. If the expectation is violated, apply the predetermined and agreed upon consequence, like grounding or taking the car keys away for a week. Consider a reward for keeping the curfew, even if it's only taking the time to brag on them. Rewards can help reinforce appropriate behavior.

Consistency between Mom and Dad

Consistency between parents is very important, since a child often learns how to approach the world by observing the behavior and values of their parents. When both parents send a unified message, a clear path is established. Parenting is a team sport. We come into marriage with all kinds of parenting ideas and philosophies shaped by our own family's culture and traditions. How we grew up is what we consider to be correct, and it can be an obstacle for a parent to change, compromise, or bend.

The group of three things that couples fight about most is called PMS: Parenting, Money and Sex. It makes a lot of sense that parenting is in this group because what's more precious to a parent than their child?

When it comes to discipline, most parents would agree that

they find themselves arguing about their differences on how, when, what's too much, and what's too little. As much as you have in common with your spouse, there's a good chance you have different parenting styles. We all enter marriage with our own belief systems, but it doesn't always mean ours are the best way. Another stumbling block is a lack of communication on the topic. Couples often make sure they're on the same page with religion, politics, and other important topics before getting married. But, most couples never talk about the kind of parent they want to be, and what they believe about discipline, until they are faced with a defiant child.

Working together to set goals for the future of your child is the result of your parenting. This means there must be clear communication between the two of you on what your beliefs are in raising your child. Discussing the differences will help you see areas of commonality, and not only the areas that conflict with your spouse. Sit down in a relaxed calm environment together to discuss how you were raised and what you want to carry over into your relationship with your kids. It will become clear how different your family backgrounds may have been, but it helps bring clarity on why your spouse thinks and reacts the way he or she does.

Here are some possible questions to help get the communication started:

- What are the good and bad memories you have of your childhood?
- What values do we want to instill in your child?

- What kinds of things would we like our children to accomplish?
- What character traits would we like to see our children develop?
- What type of discipline should be used?
- When we disagree, what's our game plan to meet in the middle?
- How do we add a strong spiritual component to our daily home life?
- What do we hope for them when they are eighteen and leaving home?
- What kind of a relationship do we want to have with them when they are preschool, grade school, middle school, high school, and as young adults?

As you work on finding common ground, do your best to uphold the decisions you agreed upon. Work hard behind the scenes to become united on your parenting strategies.

For instance:

- Don't contradict each other in front of the children.
- Don't override a decision that has just been made by the other parent.
- Don't tell the children that the other parent is wrong.
- Don't undermine the other parent in front of the kids.

Consistency in Our Daily Routines

We hear it all the time that kids need routine. We hear it from our pediatrician, our mother-in-law, our child's teacher, and our best friend. What's the big deal? Are routines truly necessary for children? Simply put, yes. Routines involve repetition. Repetition produces predictability. Predictability leads to stability. Stability provides security.

Consistency in daily and weekly routines becomes one of the most important elements of a child's life. The routine for getting out of bed and getting ready in the morning should be predictable. The after-school routine and the order in which it happens should be the same, such as an after-school snack, homework, free time, an athletic practice, and dinner. Keeping a regular and consistent routine gives children structure and teaches them the discipline of organization.

All successful people have one thing in common: healthy routines. Just as you have a routine every morning on your way out the door to work, your child needs a routine too. Being a consistent and predictable parent will make life better for your children and your family. Making clear and consistent expectations can bring order to your child's world.

Let me give you a very practical and simple way to create family consistency. It's so important to keep it as simple as possible. For instance, write down the main house rules you want lived out each day and review them often as a family. This is effective because then it isn't up to imagination or memory.

Here are some examples:

- What time is bed time?
- What time is homework time?
- What time are household chores?
- What time is curfew?
- What are the rewards?
- What are the consequences?

I advise you to write these out and recite them out loud to yourself every morning. Some will absolutely think that's unnecessary. But, the concept of rehearsal is to reinforce your new rules. The day will come when you don't need to read your list out loud, because you'll be living it. It's a simple tool but a major help in in leading your home in consistency.

George Foreman is a two-time world heavyweight boxing champion and an Olympic gold medalist. He lived by the mantra that champions don't become champions in the ring, but they're merely recognized as champions there. If you want to see if someone will develop into a champion, simply look at their daily routine. Anyone can map out a fight plan, but when you climb into the ring and the action begins, you're down to nothing but your trained reflexes. That's where the training shows up. If you cheated on that in the dark of the morning, you'll be exposed in the bright lights of the ring.

Boxing is a great analogy for leadership. Leadership rises and falls on daily routine. We succeed or fail by daily consistent routines. This is what's interesting: you can be anything you want to be through a daily routine. It's the power of focus! This needs to permeate into our jobs, finances, marriage, and children. Parents, we can't be great until God is the consistent focus of each day.

There is no shortage of men who are saying, "I don't know how to be a father. I don't know how to be a husband. I never had an example to show me what it looks like." There is an abundance of men who are unkind, rude, lack integrity, and are willing to consider divorce as an option if things get too bad. Most of the time, these men are simply repeating learned destructive patterns in areas of life that could bring them the greatest fulfillment. Allowing ourselves to believe we're not good fathers or good husbands because we didn't have a good example is the biggest lie we could believe.

When we go out on our own to pursue a career, we might know nothing about that career. But we attend a university or a training school. We study and take tests. We start as an apprentice or assistant. Over time we learn the skills to become an expert in our vocation. How? By daily consistency. Every day we choose the life we live. And, we choose what kind of parent we will be. Wise people choose wisely their daily routine, and it determines their quality and enjoyment of their life.

The other day I was sitting in a waiting room and I noticed a business magazine laying on top of a stack of magazines. It purported that consistency is the number one discipline to be successful. I truly believe that. Consistency is that pattern of behavior that distinguishes excellence from mediocrity. No one, no matter how gifted or talented, will achieve their potential without it. Consistency leads to desired consequences faster than anything else.

I recently had a delicious meal at a restaurant. I couldn't stop talking about. I told everybody and invited friends to go with me for an amazing meal. We sat down and I told them what to order. I couldn't wait until they experienced this amazing cuisine. So, we ordered. But, the outcome was vastly different! It was not nearly as good, it wasn't cooked the same, it didn't look the same, and it didn't taste the same. I was so disappointed. I haven't been back to that restaurant. What a simple, but powerful, reminder of the importance of consistency.

SECTION 3

Five Characteristics of a Generational Leader

In this section, I want to give you five biblical accounts that will assist you in impacting your children's future. Within these stories, we find five traits that can build them into generational leaders. These five traits are Confidence, Honor, Integrity, Courage, and Vision. The Bible shows us a profoundly powerful way to mold our children by these miraculous stories. By telling these stories repeatedly, you will generate passion and excitement in your children, and plant the Word of God in them.

The Power of Storytelling

There is something powerful about storytelling, and we need to utilize it as an amazing training tool within our homes. Since humans first walked the earth, long before they used the written word, they told stories. Whether through cave drawings, sitting around a fire, or under a tree, humans have told stories as a way to shape their culture. Ancient storytellers were regarded as leaders, spiritual guides, teachers, setting tribal customs, telling of heroic events, or entertainers. Storytelling came in various forms of creativity including songs, poetry, chants, and dance.

A good storyteller could easily find an audience, eager to devour every exciting bit of information in their captivating stories. These stories were also shared with others in faraway lands. When people traveled, the stories traveled with them. When they returned home, they brought with them exciting new tales of exotic places and people. In fact, sharing stories is as natural to human beings as eating and sleeping! Some of the stories we tell today have been passed down from generation to generation, while others are new ones that we create ourselves.

Jesus also utilized this amazing tool on many occasions. Matthew 13:3 notes, "Then [Jesus] told them many things in parables." Parables are often described as stories with spiritual principles. They are a means of illustrating profound, divine truths.

When we hear a story, our ability to remember details increases, because we can envision each character, and we find ourselves somewhere in the story. Jesus implemented many analogies in his stories using common things that would be familiar to everyone (salt, bread, sheep, dirt, a coin, a child), so his stories would come alive.

Storytelling captivates our children spiritually and morally with truths that will never be forgotten. Remember that your voice and gestures are your main tools! Use them to create pictures in children's minds by using interesting and expressive words, or facial expressions like scowling to show how angry a character is. Use gestures, like stretching out your arms to show how wide something is. Use different sounding voices, like a soft voice for a shy character, or a booming voice for the champion of the story.

> *What's the best way to make people feel?*
> *By telling a compelling story.*

Making time to tell your children stories can be fun and satisfying for everyone. It also lets your children know that you value spending time with them, and you're creating memories they will never forget. Storytelling is a great way to teach children the life lessons you want them to learn. Great stories allow children to explore and think about love, hate, jealousy, kindness, power, evil, and good. Storytelling stimulates children's imaginations, and can transport and connect them to the lives of biblical people. It helps connect them to you as well. Those moments will never be forgotten by your kids. But most of all, if you enjoying telling a story, there is a good chance that your kids will enjoy listening to it! And at that moment, you've taken on the effective role as their spiritual trainer.

When we utilize story-telling, sharing biblical truths, and repetition, we powerfully shape our children and their future. We all are very aware how our kids will watch the same Disney movies repeatedly. Our grandkids can sing every song from every Disney movie that has ever been made. They never tire of the same stories.

CHAPTER 7

Characteristic 1 – Confidence

Our oldest son, Dustin, loved playing baseball. He started at the age of five playing T-Ball. He played baseball with the same group of kids all the way up to high school. Between the summer of his eighth and ninth grade year, many of these boys began to grow rapidly and some developed faster than others.

At the first day of practice for the new baseball season, we pulled into the parking space facing the practice field. I turned off the car and we both stared out the window at his teammates. It was shocking how much some of them had changed physically in one year. Some were walking around with sleeveless shirts and they had muscular definition. A couple of them had facial hair. Some looked like grown men.

Dustin seemed to be in no hurry to get out of the car. That's when he turned to me and said, "Dad, I've been thinking, I really don't want to play baseball anymore." I was shocked, and responded, "What do you mean you don't want to play?

You've been talking about how you could hardly wait for baseball season. This is your favorite sport!" He responded with frustration in his voice, "I don't want to play, let's go home!"

I immediately detected that this had become an extremely intimidating moment that stirred up all kinds of personal insecurities. He felt like he could not measure up. Everyone else seemed bigger, stronger, and more talented. He was convinced he could not compete at this level, and all the other players would make fun of him. Dustin felt that walking away would be a lot easier than walking onto that field. He was willing to forfeit a love and passion all because of the fear of failing.

As a parent, I was fully aware and sensitive to his very real, internal battle of intimidation. However, I also knew this was a battle worth facing and fighting. When I saw the fear and intimidation in his eyes, my heart ached for him, because I knew all too well that sickening feeling of not measuring up. I also was unwilling for him to set a trend in his life of walking away whenever he found himself in a challenging, fearful, or intimidating situation. This is one of the greatest factors in a person's life that can keep them from accomplishing greater things.

I looked at Dustin and said, "We're not going home and you're not quitting. So, let's both get out of the car and walk out there together." This ignited a war between us. His response was strong and determined. He was not playing and he was not getting out of the car.

As a father and leader, I was determined that intimidation was not going to rule my son's life and steal this love and passion from him. In our war of words, I finally came to the place where I said firmly, "Dustin get out of the car now! If you don't, I will come to your side of the car, throw you over my shoulder and carry you to the field. There are only two options: you can walk out there or be carried out there." I got out of the car and started walking around to his side and he quickly jumped out of the car. He was furious at me for my lack of understanding as he marched to the field.

Several weeks later, Kay and I were sitting in the stands watching one of his games. He came up to bat at a critical point of the game. His team was down a couple of runs, and there were two men on base with two outs. Dustin was up to bat. As he stepped up to the plate, Kay and I were wringing our hands nervously, knowing the game could end with him.

The ball came sizzling across the plate, Dustin swung the bat, and connected with the ball. The ball rocketed high toward center field, everyone in the stands came to their feet, and we watched it clear the fence for a home run. It was the first time he had ever hit one out of the park. I'll never forget as he rounded third base coming home and his teammates ran onto the field mobbing him as the hero of the game. That season was his best and most enjoyable of all the years he played.

Confidence is a gigantic force in our kid's life. We as parents must stand on the wall of our castle as a night watchman looking over our children. We must respond immediately to the enemy called "insecurity" that desires to destroy their confidence, and ultimately keeps them from their God-given purpose.

Experts say that having positive self-esteem has a strong

correlation to good behavior and happiness, so teaching a child to have confidence is important. There is such a strong parallel between how your child feels about themselves and how they act, so it is vital to make this your focus in their formative years. No person is one-dimensional. Each individual can be seen through three different viewpoints. One is the view that others have of us: opinions. Another is the view that we have of ourselves: perception.

> *The most important is the view God has of us: reality.*

How we internalize these three views will determine for the most part, how we live out our lives. These three views shape us emotionally, spiritually, and socially.

Turkey Pecking

Turkey farmers say that if a turkey gets wounded or has a small bloody sore, the other turkeys will peck at the spot. The wound gets larger as the other turkeys are attracted to the sore spot. They keep pecking and pecking until they peck the wounded turkey to death. Turkeys are so ignorant; they keep pecking at another turkey's wound until they destroy it.

Similarly with people, when we want to understand the sinfulness of mankind or how deeply deprived we are as humans, simply visit an elementary or middle school.

By nature, kids can be mean to each other. If a fellow student is viewed as sub-par, has a weakness, or is different in some way, they will zero in on them like a flock of turkeys. They will pick at them, laugh at them, isolate them, bully them, and label them with cruel names. Unfortunately, kids believe what their peers say and this can wound them deeply.

> *Wounded children grow into wounded adults, and wounded adults will never fulfill God's call upon their life.*

Maybe this is the reason why there are so many emotionally unstable and socially-inept people. If we want to be well-rounded in all areas of life, we need to guard ourselves from harsh words and negative opinions, while staying focused on how our creator views us.

This seems to be the mindset of David when he wrote these words. Psalm 139:13–16 states, "For you created my inmost being; you knit me together in my mother's womb. I praise you because I am fearfully and wonderfully made; your works are wonderful, I know that full well. Your eyes saw my unformed body; all the days ordained for me were written in your book before one of them came to be."

Even after reading this amazing passage that reminds us of how we are created for greatness, we can struggle believing it to be true, because all we can see is our own glaring weaknesses. We believe our weaknesses stop us from achieving great things in life. However, rarely do our weaknesses ever stop us.

> *What stops us is the fear of failure. To put it more accurately, it's the fear of having our weaknesses exposed before others.*

We can't bear the thought of being embarrassed, or others thinking less of us, or being mocked. We often won't attempt things that seem difficult to us, because of the possibility of embarrassing ourselves. Remember how Dustin didn't want to get out of the car that first day of baseball practice? His highlight season could have been missed by yielding to the enemy of intimidation. In life, a baseball game doesn't have significant consequences, but learning to fight and win against intimidation is a lesson everyone needs to learn. Confidence elevates us and takes us places we could have never dreamed.

There is a story often told about how Babe Ruth once met a young boy in the hospital with a terminal illness. He asked the boy if he could do anything for him. The little boy asked Babe Ruth to hit a home run the next night. Babe Ruth stepped to the plate that next night with a bold confidence and deliberately pointed with the bat where that ball was going. The pitch was thrown and Ruth crushed the ball as it came across the plate. It went exactly where he had pointed, over the wall, for a home run.

Our kids and grandkids are waiting for someone to point them in a direction they should go. Make sure you're the one who is pointing. If you don't communicate to your children about developing bold confidence and not listening to the destructive force of insecurity, who will?

Opinions

We all form opinions of one another within seconds of meeting someone. People have opinions of you and you have opinions of them. But that's all it is: an opinion. Opinions carry no weight and have no power to alter your life, unless you allow that person to be judge over your life. Allowing someone to determine your worth is totally ridiculous, as is allowing their opinion to determine how you feel about yourself. No one can judge you, unless you grant him or her that power. Why would we allow an ordinary person to put on a judge's robe and give them such power? When we allow our worth to be determined by what others think, we are signing up for a roller coaster ride of insecurity and instability.

We long to know we matter to others, but more importantly, we need to know we matter to God. We desire approval from our peers, but we forget we already have approval from God. When our goal becomes being admired, envied, and accepted by humans, it will always lead to extreme unhappiness. It produces an empty feeling of not being good enough or the inability to measure up.

Let me give you a vivid example. Kathy Ormsby was an honor student at North Carolina State University, and the collegiate record holder in the woman's ten-thousand-meter run. The day came when she had at last achieved her dream to run in the NCAA Track Championship. Although she was favored to win, she fell behind and could not catch the eventual winner. In a startling and tragic move, she ran off the track, out of the stadium and jumped of a bridge. She survived, but was paralyzed for the rest of her life. Listening to the voices of our critics can easily lead to our demise. After all, the sinful purpose of insecurity is to destroy our purpose in life.

The Good Side of Failure

We, as a society, have believed a horrendous lie that says if we fail, we have no worth. Our culture is obsessed with how others think of us. We must have the approval of others to feel good about ourselves. Giving weight to others' opinions will become your reality. However, a lot of our life is made up of failing. You will not be good at anything until you are willing to fight through the failure stage when attempting something new. Failing is not fun.

> *Failure is frustrating, discouraging, and embarrassing. But it's the only way to rise from average to exceptional.*

Here is a great phrase to instill into our kids: failure is always the precursor of the phenomenal! I love that phrase. It broadens our perspective. With that perspective, we don't view failure as the end, but as the beginning of something phenomenal.

Approval Addicts

Many people today suffer from an unhealthy need for affirmation and struggle to feel good about themselves. For some, the quest for approval becomes an actual addiction. People who are constantly seeking self-worth from the outside world because they can't find it within themselves are setting themselves up for a myriad of difficulties.

It's well documented that everyone needs to feel appreciated on a regular basis. This stems from our human need to know that our existence has purpose and meaning. Recognition prompts our brains to release the feel-good chemical, dopamine, that we all crave and enjoy even though the high may be extremely short lived. Feeling appreciated is a healthy and positive thing we all love to receive, but when it becomes a "be-all, end-all" need in our life, it becomes dangerous.

Here's the problem: the need to seek out approval and acceptance from others can cause you to forfeit your own dreams. Your whole life becomes a part of trying to fit into everybody else's lifestyle instead of developing your own unique lifestyle. Even if you get approval from the outside, if you do not feel good about yourself on the inside, you will still feel empty.

Insecurity is prevalent among teens because they experience so many changes at this stage of life: physically, hormonally, socially, and spiritually. Everything is a new experience leaving them feeling insecure and fragile. Most fall into the trap that the approval of others measures our worth. This can continue into adulthood where we feel the need to impress others with our lifestyle. Making one more sale, getting one more raise or promotion, or achieving one more award becomes the end goal. People want to buy a bigger home, a bigger boat, a more impressive car, and they want to post every amazing detail on Instagram. Why? Because we have this secret desire inside to be envied, and somehow we equate that with success. It becomes so important that we will sacrifice God and family for position and money. That's the cultural lie we cannot let our children grow up believing.

No matter where we are in life, when we play to an audience to find our worth, we'll never measure up. The audience will always be fickle. We may receive applause today and jeers tomorrow. We may succeed today while people chant our name, but fail tomorrow and experience their mocking and rejection.

Do You Have an Approval Addiction?

- If you are hurt deeply when people express anything less than glowing opinions about your accomplishments, you could be suffering from approval addiction.
- If you constantly think that other people devalue you because of your weight, or your height, or your lack of hair, or your lack of education, you could be suffering from approval addiction.
- If you feel that to prove your own worth, you must degrade another person, you could be suffering from approval addiction.

- If you find that you always live with the nagging sense that you aren't important enough or special enough, or if you get envious of others who get the spotlight more than you do, you could be suffering from approval addiction.

The War of Insecurity

One of the saddest things I've ever experienced in ministry is being called to help a family deal with their child who had committed suicide. I've resided over too many funerals of teens ending their life because of a relational break up. The breakup was perceived as rejection, and the teen felt like he or she couldn't measure up. They are so despondent, and they end their life, because they placed their value in the hands of someone else. Numerous social media websites such as Snapchat, Facebook, Twitter, YouTube, and Instagram can add to the fire of insecurity. Every morning we step onto the social network stage where hundreds and thousands of people are following our every move. Every morning as we step back on the stage of the social spotlight, we scream, "Look at me! Look what I've done, who I'm with, and how much fun I'm having." Many times, people are making a plea to be noticed and admired.

We're consumed with following celebrities, beautiful reality stars, the rich, and the famous. The down side to this kind of obsession is that it emphasizes what we don't have, which fuels a nagging dissatisfaction.

A recent poll that was taken of fifteen-year-olds found that their number one desire in life is to be famous. After reading this, I did my own experiment with some of our grandchildren's friends at church. I saw firsthand through casual conversations with thirteen, fourteen, and fifteen-year-olds how prevalent this kind of thinking is. Their desires in life range widely. Some wanted to be dancers, singers, preachers, or writers, but the common denominator was to be famous.

This is the reason why so many people will do ridiculous things on reality television, debasing themselves simply for the prospect of being known or seen. They believe that gaining the attention of the masses is the goal in life.

A study of 1,032 sixteen-year-olds by a team of researchers in the United Kingdom determined that more than half had no desire to go into professions that didn't involve being a celebrity. Some might say this is normal and will eventually fade away, but there's a good chance these kids and others like them will take their fame pursuits into adulthood.

In a separate study conducted by the Pew Research Center among eighteen to twenty-five-year-olds, researchers found that getting rich was less important than becoming famous among young people. There are many examples online or on television of a person going from an unknown to a global sensation overnight. Young people are very aware of this.

The Chameleon Syndrome

A chameleon is a reptile that changes colors to adapt to its surroundings. This term aptly describes someone who changes who they are depending on who they're around. We want so badly to have other people's approval that we will compromise our beliefs, morals, ethics, and standards to fit in. A chameleon doesn't hold any solid convictions about anything. Their opinion simply becomes the same opinion of the person they want to impress. We find ourselves agreeing with everyone else and afraid to voice our own beliefs. We may start out disagreeing with the majority but find it's too uncomfortable to stand alone. The chameleon will shift their opinions, depending on who they are around. This happens not only with opinions, but also with our character and our personal appearance, as we attempt to fit in. People try to look like others, talk like others, and act like others so they will be liked.

> *That's when we lose our true identity, but the sadder truth is that we lose our purpose. It's the chameleon syndrome.*

Isaiah 2:22 reads, "Stop trusting in mere humans...why hold them in esteem?" What would happen if we could teach our children that the only person who determines our worth is God?

Ephesians 2:10 is powerful, "For we are God's handiwork, created in Christ Jesus to do good works, which God prepared in advance for us to do." God gave you existence and purpose, and He has a plan for your life. We need to be like Jesus. He loved everyone, but He didn't please everyone. When Jesus was baptized in Matthew 3:17, a voice from heaven spoke, "This is my Son, whom I love; with Him I am well pleased." But there were plenty of people who were not pleased with Jesus.

Jesus didn't seek their approval. He only sought the approval of his Father. When Jesus was on the Mount of Transfiguration, a voice from heaven spoke again. Mark 9:7 states, "This is my Son, whom I love. Listen to him!" God expressed his love for his son Jesus, but at the same time there were plenty of people who were angry at Jesus. They turned on Him and didn't want to listen to Him.

They claimed that Jesus was demon-possessed. Peter denied Him. The authorities arrested Him for blasphemy, but Jesus didn't allow the opinions of men to dictate his future. Instead, He continued the course He was called to fulfill. Jesus sets a great example of being secure in who He was and whom God said He was. That gave Him the strength not to bend to the desires of others.

Most parents have experienced heart-warming moments when their kids played sports. I experienced it with all three of our boys. When one of them made a great play, such as shooting a three pointer, hitting a home run, or making a spectacular catch, they came running off the field as their teammates congratulated them, giving them high fives. But, they pushed through the crowd, seemingly oblivious to all their teammates until their eyes met mine. I knew they enjoyed the attention from their teammates, but they were playing for an audience of one. All that mattered was that I was there! In life, it is enjoyable to receive pats on the back, awards for accomplishments, but in the end, all that matters is pleasing God.

> *This is the choice we are faced with. You can let others define you, or you can let your Creator define you.*

The Story of Moses

Moses was born in Egypt in the year 2368 B.C. This was a time when the Israelites were slaves to the rulers of the land and subject to many harsh decrees. Moses was the third born of three children, after Miriam and Aaron. At a young age, Moses' mother spared his life when a decree had been made for all Israelite children two-years-old and younger to be killed. She placed him in a basket, put him in the Nile river, and watched it float downstream. He was found by Pharaoh's daughter. She was captivated by him the moment she saw him. He was eventually adopted as Pharaoh's own son. He emotionally lived in two worlds. He lived in an Egyptian palace and was educated in Egyptian schools, but he had the heart of a Hebrew.

For years, he watched the mistreatment of the Jews under the whip of the slavemasters. Moses found himself walking often among the slaves because he knew he was one of them, yet they hated him, because they saw him as an Egyptian. One day, Moses walked by a slavemaster brutally beating a slave. He was so angered by what he saw, he killed the Egyptian slavemaster. He had committed a capital offense, and he knew he would be executed for the crime. He fled to the desert, married a nomad girl, and spent the next forty years there. Moses lived with his father-in-law, Jethro, and kept Jethro's sheep. One day when he was eighty-years-old, he was walking through the desert, and encountered a bush on fire.

Exodus 3:1–10 reads,

> Now Moses was tending the flock of Jethro his father-in-law, the priest of Midian, and he led the flock to the far side of the wilderness and came to Horeb, the mountain of God. There the angel of the Lord appeared to him in flames of fire from within a bush. Moses saw that though the bush was on fire it did not burn up. So Moses thought, "I will go over and see this strange sight—why the bush does not burn up." When the Lord saw that he had gone over to look, God called to him from within the bush, "Moses! Moses!" And Moses said, "Here I am." The Lord said, "I have indeed seen the misery of my people in Egypt. I have heard them crying out because of their slave drivers, and I am concerned about their suffering. So now, go. I am sending you to Pharaoh to bring my people the Israelites out of Egypt."

But Moses gives God every excuse why he can't do what God has for him to do:

- He says he doesn't feel worthy (Exodus 3:11–12).
- He says he doesn't even know God's name (Exodus 3:13–14).
- He says the Israelites will not believe him (Exodus 4:1–9).
- He says that he is not good at speaking (Exodus 4:10–12).
- He says, "Send someone else" (Exodus 4:13–17).

Moses is battling a serious case of insecurity. Notice how God deals with Moses' insecurities. It's the opposite of how we would try to help someone like him. We might start by reinforcing Moses with positive thoughts. We might help him discover his inner strength. We might say, "Moses, look into the mirror and repeat after me, 'My name is Moses. I am strong, I am confident, I am brave!'" Or, we might try to help him overcome his insecurities by telling him to close his eyes and visualize walking into Pharaoh's court, speaking to him with boldness and authority. That was not God's tactic. In fact, God didn't do any of those things. God didn't try to build up Moses' self-confidence. He knew Moses needed something more than what was in himself already. Moses needed "God-fidence."

Notice what God does say in Exodus 4:12, "Now go; I will help you…" This had nothing to do with Moses, but everything to do with God. Our help, strength and ability comes from God. Real confidence doesn't come from a better assessment of ourselves, but a clearer view of who God is. Moses continues to talk about his deficiencies in Exodus 4:13, "But Moses said, 'Pardon your servant, Lord. Please send someone else.'" God ignores Moses' request and spends the next nine verses focusing entirely on what He has done, is doing, and will do for him. He conveys to Moses that it is not about having specific abilities. It's about being available. God didn't need Moses to be a victor, He needed him to be a vessel.

Exodus 3:13–14 are the key verses, "Moses said to God, 'Suppose I go to the Israelites and say to them, "The God of your fathers has sent me to you," and they ask me, "What is his name?" Then what shall I tell them?' God said to Moses, 'I AM who I AM.' This is what you are to say to the Israelites: 'I AM has sent me to you.'" In other words, God is not like anything Moses had ever experienced. God doesn't have needs. God doesn't require any help. God doesn't get tired. God has no limits. God does not have a beginning, and God does not have an end. God is unchanging, always and forever the same. God is not intimidated by Pharaoh, God is not intimidated by the grandness of Egypt, and God is not intimidated by their gods.

Our confidence doesn't come from trying to dig deep inside of ourselves to find courage. It comes from having a better assessment of God who dwells in us. The burning bush was more than a divine pyrotechnic display. Rather, it gives us a glimpse of God's eternal, self-sustaining nature. The fire burned continually in the bush without burning up the bush. Fires need fuel, and when they consume the fuel, they go out. The fire Moses saw, however, was self-sustaining. It didn't require anything.

In the same way, God is the eternal "I AM" that needs no external fuel. Nothing precedes Him, nothing sustains Him, and nothing contains Him. When the eternal "I AM," is on your side, you don't need anything else.

In the New Testament, Jesus takes this "I AM" name and applies it to our greatest areas of brokenness and need:

- To those who hunger, Jesus says, "I am the bread of life" (John 6:35).
- To those who thirst, Jesus says, "I am the living water" (John 7:38–39).
- To those in darkness, Jesus says, "I am the light" (John 8:12).
- To those who need a fresh start, Jesus says, "I am the door" (John 10:9).
- To those who feel abandoned, Jesus says, "I am the Good Shepherd" (John 10:11).
- To those who feel lost, Jesus says, "I am the way" (John 14:6).
- To those confused, Jesus says, "I am the truth" (John 14:6).
- To those afraid of death, Jesus says, "I am the life" (John 14:6).
- To the dead Jesus says, "I am the resurrection" (John 11:25).

These are the things Jesus wants to be to you. Our kids need to know this and understand it. These "I AM" sayings aren't simply nice creative names for God. It describes to our children, in extreme detail, who God is in their personal life. Truly understanding this will bring deep confidence into our lives. Insecurity is a satanic disease that destroys what God created. It lies to you about your identity. Insecurity is one of the most debilitating forces in human life. Our kids need to understand where insecurity and true confidence comes from. The enemy wants to stop you and God wants to advance you.

The Baby Eagle and The Chickens

There is an amazing story recounted by Jamie Green in her book, *Walk Tall: You're a Daughter of God.* She writes,

> A fable is told about an eagle who thought he was a chicken. When the eagle was very small, he fell from the safety of his nest. A chicken farmer found the eagle, brought him to the farm, and raised him in a chicken coop among his many chickens. The eagle grew up doing what chickens do, living like a chicken, and believing he was a chicken. A naturalist came to the chicken farm to see if what he had heard about an eagle acting like a chicken was really true. He knew that an eagle is king of the sky. He was surprised to see the eagle strutting around the chicken coop, pecking at the ground, and acting very much like a chicken. The farmer explained to the naturalist that this bird was no longer an eagle. He was now a chicken because he had been trained to be a chicken and he

believed that he was a chicken. The naturalist knew there was more to this great bird than his actions showed as he "pretended" to be a chicken. The man lifted the eagle onto the fence surrounding the chicken coop and tried to make him fly. The eagle moved slightly, only to look at the man; then he glanced down at his home among the chickens in the chicken coop where he was comfortable. He jumped off the fence and continued doing what chickens do. The farmer was satisfied. "I told you it was a chicken," he said. The naturalist returned the next day and took the eagle to the top of the farmhouse and tried again but the eagle jumped from the man's arm onto the roof of the farmhouse. The naturalist returned again the next morning and took the eagle and the farmer some distance away to the foot of a high mountain. They could not see the farm nor the chicken coop from this new setting. The man held the eagle on his arm and pointed high into the sky where the bright sun was beckoning. This time the eagle stared skyward into the bright sun, straightened his large body, stretched his massive wings, slowly at first, then surely and powerfully. With the mighty screech of an eagle, he flew.

I love this story because we can see ourselves in it so clearly.

> *There is something far greater in you*
> *than you could possibly imagine!*

This is exactly what God was showing Moses. In this Old Testament story, God reveals three things Moses held in his hand that will also help us overcome our feelings of inadequacies.

Moses Held His Identity in His Hand

Exodus 4:2, "Then the Lord said to him, 'What is that in your hand?' 'A staff,' he replied." When Moses looked at the object he was holding in his hand, it was nothing but a stick. This was a staff about five or six feet long, used to guide and lead sheep. That staff identified Moses as a shepherd. It labeled him. It defined him. People immediately knew who he was by the shepherd's staff he carried. Everyone is defined by something. You are identified by what you carry, or in a sense, how you carry yourself. When your name is spoken, it immediately produces an image of how you are perceived. Whether respected or disrespected, we all carry a label. What you carry, such as your actions, your words or your attitude is what will define you.

Moses Held His Past in His Hand

God asked Moses what he held in his hand. Moses answered God's question with the words, "A staff." He wasn't providing

God with new information. Rather, God was asking Moses to carefully consider the thing he held in his hand.

When God asked this question, Moses experienced a stinging reminder that he once held a scepter instead of a stick. When he lived in the palace in Egypt, he was being trained and educated to be a Pharaoh. There was a time he held the world in his hand. Now, the stick he's holding reminded him that he had nothing. He had no position, power, authority, or influence. He had gone from one extreme to the other. What he now carried, defined him.

We all carry things around such as sins, hurt feelings, anger, envy, or resentment which reminds us of painful experiences. What you carry will define you.

Moses Held His Potential in His Hand

Exodus 4:3–5, "The Lord said, 'Throw it on the ground.' Moses threw it on the ground and it became a snake… Then the Lord said to him, 'Reach out your hand and take it by the tail.'"

People who work with snakes will tell you that this is a recipe for disaster. If you are going to pick up a snake, you should always grab it behind the head. By asking Moses to pick it up by the tail, God was demonstrating that He is in complete control of our lives even when it's frightening, intimidating, and makes no sense. God took that weak, powerless, dead stick and used it as a miraculous power in the hands of Moses. What you carry will define you.

What Do You Hold in Your Hand?

Whatever you hold in your hand, whether talents, gifts, or personality, know this: if what you hold in your hand is not yielded to God, it will limit the plans God has for you. That wooden stick represented Moses' life. But God wanted to show him that he needed nothing more than God.

Many people have a poor self-image of themselves, because they focus on everything they don't like about themselves. This story reminds and encourages us that we have everything we need in our hand. We need to give it to the Lord.

God will empower and use whatever is yielded to Him. God used a wooden staff to part the Red Sea. God used a donkey to speak to a rebellious prophet. God caused the sea to become solid for Peter to walk upon it. And likewise, God will do in you what you are incapable of doing.

Protecting our Kids from Insecurity

Insecurity causes feelings of self-doubt. Be a parent that is constantly looking out for and guarding against insecurity creeping into our kids' lives and threatening their future. There is no easy way to shift a child's insecurity to confidence. But here are ten ways to improve how your child feels about themselves.

Give Them Your Time

The most important aspect of raising a confident child is giving them your time. Talk, share, laugh, and learn together.

Give them Your Affection

Children need affection from a father as much as affection from their mother. A gentle hug, a kiss on the forehead, or holding hands as you walk together shows kids you love them. In regards to child development, affection makes everything better.

Build Them Up

When we praise our children, it builds their self-esteem and self-worth. When it's warranted, always be sure to praise them loudly and proudly. Your verbal encouragement will provide the security they require to flourish.

Set Clear and Consistent Boundaries

Children test limits constantly, but when boundaries are enforced, they feel secure. Clear and consistent boundaries show your children you care for them and love them deeply.

Listen to Them

When kids are young, they have a lot to say, so when they're talking, make sure that you're listening carefully. You can learn so much about them and what they are dealing with internally. Too often in their teen years, they become closed off in their communication with their parents.

Develop communication skills early, so your kids will feel comfortable talking to you about everything and anything. This will help throughout their teen years. That level of trust benefits everyone.

Have Fun with Them

Laughter is the cure for many troubles in this world. Child behavior is based greatly on the behavior of parents. Provide them with a happy and loving home, filled with laughter and joy.

Invest in What They Love

Every child has special gifts and talents to offer the world. Our children need to know that we love them for exactly who they are. Look for what a child is good at naturally, and help him or her develop those things.

Provide Balance

Find an appropriate balance between justice and mercy. When children do the wrong thing, it's easy to want to correct them by giving a punishment or consequence. However, children also need to experience mercy. They need to know that all of us make mistakes, and they need to experience forgiveness.

Give Them Unconditional Love

When children fail, we need to be there to offer a strong hand, give them a hug, and start all over again. This is unconditional love. They should know without question that no matter what happens, you will love them.

Don't Forget God in Everyday Life

How true the phrase is, "The family that prays together stays together." There is great security in knowing that we have a God who loves us and has a great purpose for our life. Our children should be taught that we are not left alone to our own abilities, but that supernatural help and guidance is available for all who call upon our God. That provides the greatest security for our kids.

CHAPTER 8

Characteristic 2 – Honor

My mom was a school teacher. She would leave for work earlier than my dad because she had such a long drive to the school where she worked. Every morning, my dad was in the kitchen cooking breakfast for everyone. Every day started the same. He banged pots and pans, singing while he cooked. He was a horrible singer. I'd keep a pillow over my head. I would come in the kitchen, sit at the table, acting tired, grumpy, and irritable, sometimes dropping my forehead onto the table. I dreaded school, I dreaded the day, and I thought, "What a miserable day."

Noticing my misery, my dad would say, "What a great day! This is the best day of your life! This is the day the Lord has made!" I would look at him like he was from a different planet! In my opinion there was nothing good about the day. Every day was not a good day for my dad. There were many days he lived in pain. He went through three hip replacements, and always walked with a limp. If he felt it or not, he always declared, "This is a good day to be alive!"

Mom would get home from work earlier than dad, and she always had dinner ready when he got home. Without fail, she made meal time a priority. We ate at the table as a family. This was the place we always connected with each other.

Here is the scene I vividly remember: mom went out of her way to serve every member of our family by not only preparing dinner, but by showing kindness, patience, and affection for each family member. When everyone was finished eating, my dad was the first one up from the table to start doing the dishes. Many times he would say to mom, "Don't get up, sit right there and let's talk." He was the fastest dishwasher I have ever seen. At that time, I didn't understand what they were doing, but it must have impressed me, because I still remember it to this day. I can't think of anything more powerful and influential than a husband and wife who master the art of serving and honoring those in their own home. The higher the leadership, the greater the servanthood.

Matthew 20:28 gives us great insight into this concept, "… the Son of Man did not come to be served, but to serve, and to give his life as a ransom for many."

> *Serving is a discipline, serving is an act of love, and serving is honoring others.*

Who Do You Remember?

What are the moments you remember the most in your past? To be more specific, who do you remember? Well, let me tell you who you probably don't remember. You probably don't remember the names of the last five Miss America winners, the names of the last five Academy Award Winners, or the Most Valuable Players in football, basketball, and baseball last year. As big of a football fan that I am, I don't often remember who played in last year's championship game. We quickly forget so many major events and the names of those people who accomplish great things. But, you can probably remember the name of the teacher who took an interest in you when you needed help. You can name the people who helped you through a difficult time. You can name the person who led you to Christ. You can name the people who believed in you when no one else did.

Why is this the case? These are people who served you. They honored you, and honor burns a deep impression into your memory so that it's never forgotten. Our quest to raise world changers becomes impossible without developing this character trait.

What does honor mean? Whom should we give honor to? Who deserves it and who doesn't? Is honor just given to a select few heroic men and women?

The Foundation of Honor

What makes honor so powerful is its foundation. It's more than a code of conduct. Honor is the heart and character of God. He demonstrates what honor looks like. We who were His enemies, we who were orphans and beggars, naked and ashamed, have been cleansed, clothed, seated at His table, and called sons and daughters.

God knows everything about you, and loves and values you. That is honor. We honor one another because we've been honored. Honor is central to who God is and what He does, and it should be central to the life of every Christian.

We live in a culture and age of dishonor. This is a time when political cartoons, editorials, talk radio, and cable networks rip our nation's leaders to pieces. They seem to focus on destroying reputations daily. It has become so common, no one thinks about it anymore.

Every day, we are saturated by the enormous floods of attacks, slander, character assassinations, and hate for the people we disagree with, or those on the other side of the political or spiritual aisle. This extreme level of dishonor flows from the media into our own homes. Nobody is safe from attack or being dishonored, not the president, not members of congress, not school teachers, pastors, or law enforcement officers. We have quickly entered a disrespectful age where no one is off limits. Our children will pick up what we say about our leaders, and learn to dishonor anyone in authority over them. What is the standard we need to teach our children when it comes to honor? Let's start by defining it.

Honor is synonymous with esteem, respect, homage, and value. The Greek word translated "honor" is *timao*, and it means, "To revere." Showing honor means treating another person respectfully because we revere or value them highly. Again, who is due honor? Here is the answer from God's Word.

We Are to Honor One Another

Romans 12:10, "Be devoted to one another in love. Honor one another above yourselves." Paul is writing that the church should be a place of unparalleled honor. Honor must be mutually and lavishly exchanged within the church. Paul reminds us "the parts of the body that we think are less honorable, we treat with special honor" (1 Corinthians 12:23). Paul doesn't simply command us to honor each other, but to try and outdo one another in showing honor.

We Are to Honor Our Parents

The last six of the Ten Commandments deal with relationships with other people. The fifth commandment reads: "Honor your father and your mother, that your days may be long upon the land which the Lord your God is giving you" (Exodus 20:12). God states no qualifier. He does not tell us to honor our parents only if they are honorable. We must treat them with respect, simply because they are our parents.

We Are to Honor Our Children

Parents are not to provoke their children, but "bring them up in the training and admonition of the Lord" (Ephesians 6:4). Our Heavenly Father sets the example by publicly honoring His son more than once (Matthew 3:17; 17:5).

Jesus preaches on the closeness He has with His father

(John 5:18–30) and the mutual respect and honor that is present in their relationship. Our Heavenly Father honors His son and expects us to honor Him also (John 5:23). Those of us with children should take time to study this section carefully. Do we treat our children with the dignity and respect due someone made in the image of God? Luke states that how we treat our children indicates how we will lead a city.

We Are to Honor Our Wives

Peter admonishes men, "Husbands, in the same way be considerate as you live with your wives, and treat them with respect as the weaker partner and as heirs with you of the gracious gift of life, so that nothing will hinder your prayers" (1 Peter 3:7).

A husband who honors his wife should let her know she is the most amazing woman in the land. This is so much at the heart of who men should be as followers of Christ, that we must realize God will turn a deaf ear to us if we violate this command.

We Are to Honor Our Husbands

Ephesians 5:22, "Wives, submit yourselves to your own husbands as you do to the Lord." Paul reminds wives to honor their husbands as if he were Christ. That is the standard.

When children see mom honoring dad, and dad praising and honoring mom, they in turn find it so much easier to honor their father and mother. Beyond that, this powerful example teaches them how they should conduct themselves when they eventually marry and have children.

We Are to Honor the Elderly

Leviticus 19:32, "Stand up in the presence of the aged, show respect for the elderly and revere your God. I am the Lord." Again, God includes no reservations or qualifiers. We are to honor our elders as if standing in the presence of Jesus.

We Are to Honor Widows

1 Timothy 5:3, "Give proper recognition to those widows who are really in need." Widows can fall victims to abuse, because they are vulnerable and alone. They can become victims of scams. We need to identify any widows around us and give them special respect and attention.

We Are to Honor Elders and Pastors

1 Timothy 5:17, "The elders who direct the affairs of the church well are worthy of double honor, especially those whose work is preaching and teaching."

Respect for pastors and the ministry has eroded in recent years. Whether we think they have earned it or not, this position requires honor. Jesus teaches us the principle of respecting and honoring those who sit in Moses' seat, even if they are hypocritical Pharisees (Matthew 23:2–3). Pastors who are faithful, hard-working, and teach the Word of God well should be honored twice as much.

We Are to Honor Our Bosses

Bosses are often subjected to ridicule, sarcasm, cartoons, and jokes. Some ridicule may seem justified, but notice what Paul says in 1 Timothy 6:1, "All who are under the yoke of slavery should consider their masters worthy of full respect, so that God's name and our teaching may not be slandered."

While this verse specifically mentions slavery, the principle is the same: respect and honor the boss. Ephesians 6:5–8 states we should sincerely obey, respect and serve a boss as if he or she were Christ himself. In no place does Paul say our boss must first act like Christ before being given that respect.

We Are to Honor the Emperor

1 Peter 2:17, "Show proper respect to everyone, love the family of believers, fear God, honor the emperor."

In three words, Peter teaches a very difficult concept. He commands us to "Honor the emperor." The historical background of his words gives a perspective on this powerful lesson. Peter, having already written that we should honor all people, knew some brethren would resist honoring Nero, the heathen Roman emperor. Nero was a perverted madman, and was eventually hated by the Romans themselves. He mercilessly tortured and killed hundreds of Christians in cruel and demeaning ways. It is almost unimaginable to expect Nero to be honored by someone whose mother had been crucified and used as a human candle for one of Nero's garden parties! Yet, the pattern that we have seen throughout scripture surfaces again here. Nero was king. A king is to be honored, for he represents the office given him by God (Romans 13:1). Whether the king is honorable or not, he is king, and we should honor him as such.

Today in our nation, the United States presidency is more polarizing than at any time in history. All respect is gone for the office of the president. It is sad that kids will grow up thinking it is normal and acceptable to speak evil against a leader. No matter how badly an American president conducts himself, it pales to the actions of Nero. Many of the early Christians no doubt despised Nero's reckless, godless behavior. Some had personal reasons to hate him. The command to honor the king, however, remained the same: forgive those who trespass against you (Matthew 6:14).

Jesus proclaimed, "But I tell you, love your enemies, and pray for those who persecute you" (Matthew 5:44). Honor the king.

We Are to Honor All People

It should be clear that honoring goes way beyond simply respecting God and parents. God wants a world where the respect and honor of others is the way of life of its citizens. We are to honor one another, but do we? We should challenge ourselves to think of ways to show honor to someone, every day. Imagine a world where everyone honors everyone else!

Parents, set the right tone of honor in your home. We may strongly disagree with our leaders and be displeased with their moral and spiritual behavior, but we at no time have the right to speak evil against anyone. We honor because God first honors us.

When we give honor, we are acting like our Lord! The standard within our homes should be, "We are people of honor."

Obedience vs. Honor

Most parents recognize the value of teaching their children how to obey, but few teach their children the art of honor. Let me show you the difference between obedience and honor. Obedience is doing what someone says, right away, without being asked again. It is learning to do a task by following directions. Honor means to treat people as special, doing more than what's expected, and having a good attitude while doing so.

> *If you want your children to do right, teach them obedience. If you want them to have great success in life, teach them to honor others.*

Ephesians 6:1–3 states, "Children, obey your parents in the Lord, for this is right. 'Honor your father and mother' — which is the first commandment with a promise — 'so that it may go well with you and that you may enjoy long life on the earth.'" This passage lays out two of the aspects of leadership development for our children: obedience and honor. Thus, obedience is fulfilling a task and getting a job done. Honor addresses how well the job is done.

How many times have we watched our kids walk past unmade beds, stepped over dirty clothes on the floor, or walked past dirty dishes in the sink. It's easy for them to think, "I didn't make the mess and it's not my responsibility. I will only do what has been required of me and nothing more." We justify that kind of thinking because no one told me that it was my job to clean it up. That is true when we solely focus on obedience. But, honor adds a deeper dimension to our relationships. Honor sees a need and meets it no matter who made the mess. Honor is taking the opportunity to value others. The goal is not to get kids to act or do something correctly, but also to think correctly.

Honor goes deeper than an act of outward obedience. The act of honoring others goes beneath the surface and resides deep in their heart. It's a spiritual trait that every child should be taught because the core issue in our children is selfishness that must be addressed and redacted. Obedience can produce the right action but not always the right attitude. It's the reason that changing someone's behavior isn't enough. We must appeal to the heart of caring and loving others. Most parents see wrong behavior and use a form of discipline to get their child to do what is right. They think at this point, the discipline is complete. That's not always true. The child may fulfill a task, and produce the right behavior, but they may be filled with anger and resentment. The goal of discipline is to help our children not only act correctly, but also think correctly. That's the beginning of honor.

Family Culture Statement

There is something about the power of the written word. I would advise every parent to create, write out and post a family culture statement. For example, this is our family mission statement:

We believe being a Woodward is special. We're not only out for ourselves. We work as a team. When a job needs to be done, the Woodward team pulls together. We work hard to clean up the house, to do yard work, to share in any needs and responsibilities, because we are a team.

A clearly written mission statement will help guard against wrong attitudes. Meanness is not acceptable because it doesn't fit our identity. Angry outbursts require an apology because hurtful words aren't consistent with the idea that we value each other. And, the Woodward team also has special privileges. We have fun as a family, go out to eat, play games, watch movies, and enjoy hanging out together. When we are together we treat each other as special. I love my family team!

Something as simple as writing out a family culture statement will give your children a clear goal of expectations. This will go a long way in shaping their character of respect and honoring others that will set them apart.

Don't fall into the deception of believing our children's negative behavior is simply a stage they'll grow out of.

Unfortunately, instead of growing out of bad patterns, children grow into them. If not counteracted, selfish habits will simply become more entrenched.

> *Here is a great way to view it: obedience brings order, honor brings peace and joy.*

Teach Our Children to Honor and Respect Each Family Member

Treating others as special does not come natural for most people and must be learned. The learning ground is in the home, and we learn by what is played out in the home every day.

How often do we come home from work and are greeted by our kids running to the front door with accusations of unfairness and meanness from their siblings? I remember it well, "Jonathan hit me," or "Brandon locked me out of my bedroom," or "Dustin is being mean to me." This is never the greeting we hope for! Everybody has an accusation but no one is at fault.

If you have multiple children, there are times we wonder if our kids are the only ones who have a constant streak of meanness in them. It's so easy and natural for all of us to gravitate towards negativity and meanness. But meanness is a violation of honor. It's the opposite of kindness and respect. Name calling, belittling, agitating one another, hitting, screaming, and yelling is not permitted, because it's a violation of who we are as a family. Say it often and say it clearly, "In this family we respect and honor one another. We never tear down, we build up. We don't stoop to unkindness or put-downs." Bad habits must be replaced with good ones. We treat people with kindness because we honor and value each other.

Find moments to teach honor. It can be as simple as setting a standard of how we greet one another as we walk in the door after a long day. How often do we walk in the door after being at work all day and walk past family members and we barely get a grunt out of them? There is no acknowledgement that we are home, and we wonder if anyone even cares. That's not a healthy environment of respect and honor. What if we greeted one another at the door like our dog greets us? Every time I come home, the dogs jump up from wherever they are and come running, jumping, and barking with extreme excitement. I realize they greatly overdo it, because I can go outside for ten minutes to take out the trash and when I walk back in the door, it's the same routine. But, there is absolutely a lesson to learn from their love and excitement for each family member.

Parents, make this a fun family standard. It's easy and its payoff is big. Here's the standard: we greet and acknowledge family members when they come in the door. Stand up, walk to the door, greet them with a smile a hug or a kiss. Ask about their day. Express that we're glad they are home, and this will undoubtedly create a stronger family bond. It's an opportunity to show honor!

When children learn honor by seeing it, they will begin to think of others first and when they do, you're way ahead of the game called parenting.

Teach Our Children to Always Go the Second Mile.

One of the marvels of the Roman Empire was a vast system of super highways that they had built for travel to and from their conquered territories. There were more than fifty thousand miles of these Roman roads throughout the Empire. At each single mile, there was a stone marker.

These mile markers pointed directions, determined the distance to the next town, warned of dangers that might lie ahead, and pointed to Rome itself. Hence the common phrase, "All roads lead to Rome."

By law, a Roman citizen or soldier could compel a subject from one of the conquered lands to carry his backpack or load for one mile, but one mile only.

As Jesus was preaching his Sermon on the Mount, I have often wondered if he inserted the reference about the second mile when he saw an object lesson unfolding before him and his listeners. He said in Matthew 5:41, "If anyone forces you to go one mile, go with them two miles." Can you imagine the bombshell this must have been as he spoke to those who were under a Roman rule that they so deeply despised and resented? Jesus called upon his hearers to do what was required of them by the Romans, and then extra.

Jesus is talking about a mindset that separates us from most others in the world. It's learning to live at a high level of honoring, and showing respect even to people who despise you. The first mile is what we call obedience. It's the thing required of us. Honor never forgets the second mile. The first is a mandated mile, the second is the miracle mile. The first mile is obligation, it's the action of common people. The second mile is the mile of honoring others. It's the action of a rare few that opens extraordinary doors that nothing else will. Honor does more than what is expected, and others take notice.

When this is taught at a young age, you will begin to see the fruit as children grow. It starts in the smallest things. One afternoon, a storm was moving in as I came through our den where Jonathan was watching TV. I asked if he could bring in the trash can from the street and put it up. He jumped up, went to the street, and rolled the trash container down the driveway to put it by the side of the garage. By this time, the wind gusts were very high. He stood there for a moment and knew the wind would blow it away. He moved it to another location where it was more secure, and stood there for a moment to make sure it wouldn't move. When I watched that at a distance, I realized he wasn't simply obeying my request, but he went a step farther in being thoughtful about the request. That's showing honor! Honor is not only doing the job; it's doing the job well.

A great practice ground for learning how to honor is around the house. For instance, early in the morning when everyone is rushing to get ready for school and work, the bathrooms are a busy place. When you finish, before you walk out, turn around and take a last look. Ask yourself if it is ready for the next family member? Did you hang up the towel, pick up dirty clothes, and shut the cabinet doors? Is the sink clean?

Obedience gets things done. Honor does things beautifully.

After dinner, there may be a schedule of whose turn it is to clean the kitchen. We may be thinking, "Thank goodness it's not my job tonight, my turn was last night." Honor isn't about whose job it is, it's about a job that must be done. Honor knows it's not my job or responsibility, but honor decides to step in, and help your brother or sister so they can finish up the dishes a little quicker. These kinds of random actions create family bonds and family peace like few ever experience. It's so easy, and it costs us so little, and the payoff is so rewarding.

Parents, if you notice your kids doing acts of honor, brag on them. Put more of your focus on what they do rather than what they don't do. Remember the principle of storytelling? This biblical account will reinforce the characteristic of honor in your children's lives.

The Story of Mephibosheth

In 2 Samuel, we encounter an interesting story. Mephibosheth was only five years old when his father, Jonathan, and grandfather, King Saul, died in the battle with the Philistines at Mt. Gilboa. It was customary that when a king was defeated and killed in battle, shame was brought on the whole kingdom. Many times, the king's family would be executed so there would be no descendent of the defeated king left to reclaim the throne. When the news that the king had been killed reached the kingdom, the family and all the king's staff fled for their lives.

Mephibosheth's nanny picked him up and fled, but in the

panic and chaos she stumbled and fell. More than likely they were trampled by the mob trying to escape. The boy was severely injured in the accident that left him crippled for the rest of his life. Many years later, when David had become king, he began to inquire about King Saul's grandson. King David and Jonathan had been very close friends, as close as brothers. Because of their relationship and an oath David made to Jonathan and to honor king Saul (1 Samuel 20:15–16, 42), he wanted to find and care for Mephibosheth.

One of Saul's servants was questioned and told King David of the young man's location. Mephibosheth was summoned to appear before the King. Though afraid, Mephibosheth came to the palace, not knowing if he would be tortured or killed. He was crippled, had lost his heritage, and lived in a desolate place named Lo Debar. Translated, that name literally means "land of nothing." Mephibosheth had been reduced to having nothing.

2 Samuel 9 describes the meeting of Mephibosheth and King David. The young man humbly bowed, and David told him to not be afraid, saying, "I will surely show you kindness for the sake of your father Jonathan. I will restore to you all the land that belonged to your grandfather Saul and you will always eat at my table" (2 Samuel 9:7). Mephibosheth was promised that his grandfather's wealth would be restored and he would always eat at the King's table. This was despite Mephibosheth's low self-worth, physical handicap, and shame brought to him by his grandfather. The story of Mephibosheth is a wonderful example of how King David showed honor to those whom the world deemed as the least and forgotten.

This is a great conversation we can begin having with our kids about who to honor and how to show honor. The only way they will establish this in their lives is by your guidance and by practicing in real-life situations.

When our youngest son, Brandon, was in elementary school, I saw this amazing trait of honoring others blossoming within him. Brandon has always had a magnetic personality and has never lacked for friends. I remember his grandmother, Mimi, and I calling him the "Underdog Hunter." He was constantly seeking out those who seemed to be rejected by the majority, or the one who was sitting alone in the school cafeteria. He befriended the one living up the street who had no friends. He included them, sat with them, and invited them to his birthday parties and to church. Those small acts of kindness brought joy and a sense of worth to those young boys who were considered outcasts and loners. Parents, teachers, coaches and grandparents took notice of how Brandon cared and showed honor to the lonely. The amazing thing about honor is this: when you honor others, honor will flow back upon you.

It elevated Brandon in the eyes of everyone who knew him. When your kids begin to show honor to others, they will stand out in the crowd. What was established in Brandon so many years ago is still one of the most attractive attributes he possesses as a young pastor. You will reap what you sow. Teach your children to sow seeds of honor in every direction, because it will come back to them in amazing ways they will never expect.

CHAPTER 9

Characteristic 3 – Integrity

This past year while our family was on vacation, we stopped at a very popular restaurant to eat. Driving up, the first thing you see is their huge sign out front: *Lambert's Cafe, Home of the Throwed Rolls*.

When we walked in, we quickly understood the meaning of their restaurant's name. As soon as we were seated, one of the wait staff yelled at us and started throwing large homemade rolls in our direction from halfway across the restaurant. As fast as these rolls were flying, they must have recruited all the high school baseball pitchers in the area to be on their wait staff.

We had a table of fifteen: Kay and I, our kids, their wives, and all the grandchildren. Hot rolls came flying from all directions and when one was caught, it made the popping sound of a baseball hitting a mitt. It started the meal with a lot of fun and excitement, and we did remarkably well, catching about 80 percent of the rolls thrown in our direction.

Then, apple-butter was served to spread on the hot rolls. It was out of this world! Servers started coming by with what they call "extras." With no extra charge, they came to the table carrying pots of fried okra, fried potatoes, macaroni, black eyed peas, and sorghum and honey. That happened even before we ordered our meal.

The one rule the restaurant had was that no one could share plates. The menu is full of good southern cooking. I ordered their famous chicken fried steak and when they brought it to the table, it was bigger than the plate it was served on. They served sides of mashed potatoes, cream gravy, spicy collard greens, and corn on the cob. When I walked out of that restaurant, I was miserable. I don't think I've ever eaten that much food at one time in my life.

Getting into the car, I said with all sincerity and a moan in my voice, "I never want to eat again in my life!" The crazy thing is that four hours later, I found myself staring into the refrigerator, hungry again.

> *An appetite can never fully be satisfied.*

Wrong Cravings

The word integrity comes from the same Latin root as the word, "integer." This is a mathematical term, meaning: a whole number; a number that is not a fraction; and a thing complete in itself. A person who walks in integrity is whole. A person of integrity is not living a divided, hypocritical life. A person of integrity is the same in private as in public.

The Bible is full of references to integrity, character, and moral purity. In 1 Kings 9:4, God instructs Solomon to walk with "integrity of heart and uprightness" as his father did. David says in 1 Chronicles 29:17, "I know, my God, that you test the heart and are pleased with integrity." In Psalm 78:70–72, we read that "David shepherded them with integrity of heart, with skillful hands."

The book of Proverbs also provides an abundance of verses on integrity. Proverbs 10:9 states, "Whoever walks in integrity walks securely, but whoever takes crooked paths will be found out." A great benefit of living a life of integrity is never having to fear being exposed. Integrity provides a safe and peaceful path through life. Another benefit is found in Proverbs 20:7, "The righteous lead blameless lives; blessed are their children after them." The parent who walks in integrity provides a path for his or her children to follow. What a great gift to pass down!

The book, *The Day America Told the Truth,* by James Patterson and Peter Kim, used a survey technique that guaranteed the privacy and anonymity of the respondents, while documenting what Americans believe and do. The results were startling.

First, they found there was no moral authority in America: "Americans are making up their own moral codes. Only 13 percent of us believe in all Ten Commandments, and 40 percent of us believe in five of the Ten Commandments. We choose which laws of God we believe in. There is absolutely no moral consensus in this country as there was in the 1950's, when all our institutions commanded more respect."

Second, they found Americans are not honest: "Lying

has become an integral part of American culture, a trait of the American character. We lie and don't even think about it. We lie for no reason." The authors estimate that 91 percent of Americans lie regularly.

Third, marriage and family are no longer sacred institutions. "While we still marry, we have lost faith in the institution of marriage. A third of married men and women confessed to us that they've had at least one affair." The authors conclude by suggesting that we have a new set of commandments.

Note how Americans responded to some of these key commandments:

- I don't see the point in observing the Sabbath (77 percent).
- I will steal from those who won't really miss it (74 percent).
- I will lie when it suits me, so long as it doesn't cause any real damage (64 percent).
- I will cheat on my spouse; after all, given the chance, he or she will do the same (53 percent).

However, what is fascinating is that we want to hold everybody around us to a high standard of integrity. We want our mechanic to be trustworthy, our politicians to live by a strict moral and ethical code, and our spouse to be faithful. We desire for everyone we encounter and do business with to treat us respectfully and honestly. Apparently, we don't have the same set of standards for ourselves.

The great deception is that we believe it's fine to be dishonest a little bit. We say we want to be people of integrity, but believe there's no problem with telling our boss a small lie to get a day off. We say we want to be honest, but then cheat on our taxes. We say we want to follow God's word, yet refuse to be generous with our finances which fuels the message of Christ to a world that desperately needs to hear. We want to be a person people trust, but do or say unethical things to make one more sale. We ease our conscience by telling ourselves it's not that big of a deal.

Think of the story about the man who sent a letter to the Internal Revenue Service. He said, "I cheated on my income taxes, and felt so bad that I couldn't sleep. Enclosed you will find a check for one hundred dollars. And if I still can't sleep, I'll send the rest of what I owe."

Many of us can relate to that man. We want to be honest, but sometimes we find it easier to be dishonest. So, we try to find a way to compromise our values so that a little bit of deception doesn't bother our conscience.

In this chapter I want to talk about appetites. Appetite can be defined as "a strong desire or urge." While we typically associate it with food or drink, this word refers to any powerful wish, including the longing for security, a craving for wealth, or a sexual desire. Most of our appetites, in their purest forms, are God-given. The problem arises when we allow them to get out of control and pursue cravings that are destructive both physically and spiritually. Remember, a person of integrity is living rightly, not divided, nor being a different person in different circumstances. Integrity will keep our appetites in check.

Too many times I have found myself sitting across from someone weeping uncontrollably saying, "I would have never believed my life would have turned out like this!" In most cases the devastation they are experiencing is self-imposed. They indulged in a foolish or sinful action that brought about enormous repercussions. Nobody sets out to destroy their life but it happens all the time. This happens even to the most brilliant and extremely talented, because of a wrong decision. Choices contain tremendous power that determine the quality of life you will live. This is an area we cannot get wrong. This is another foundational principal our children must fully grasp.

Think about your own life for a moment. You might have been born with good or poor genetics. You might have been born into a rich family or a poor one. You might have been raised in a toxic environment or a healthy one. These are all things you had no control over. You didn't choose your talents, skin color, or parents. You didn't even choose your own name.

Fortunately, there is another part of the equation. We do have control over how we will live out our lives. We can live under the protective hand of God, being an amazing parent or a kind, loving spouse. We can be a contributor instead of a consumer in society. We can live in peace instead of turmoil. The equation to a successful or disappointing life is simply the total of our past choices. No matter where you start off in life, good choices lead to a better life and bad choices lead to a lower quality of life. We cannot afford to make mistakes with something that determines our destiny. Our choices have a great impact on our lives. The good news is that we have complete and total control over every decision we make.

We have all developed certain cravings and appetites for various things such as food, caffeine, sweets, alcohol, drugs, sex, fame, or money. It's a never-ending list. It's important to note that we never outgrow cravings and they never go away, not even at the age of thirty, forty, or sixty. Success in life is determined by our ability to manage appetites and not be controlled by them.

Again, let me emphasize the purpose behind storytelling. These are not simply old fables, but every Bible story has a purpose to help us, as parents, in the vital job of teaching and training our children to change their world.

The Story of Esau and the Bowl of Stew

This story is about an out-of-control appetite that led to disaster. The story begins in Genesis 25 where we find two twin brothers, Jacob and Esau. Esau was a rugged outdoors man, a hunter and protector type. Jacob was more of a mama's boy. He spent more time indoors, learning to cook, and helping his mom around the house. They were twins, but complete opposites.

Esau was born first, therefore he rightfully owned the birthright. The birthright becomes the centerpiece of this story. The custom was that the oldest son would receive the birthright, which included a double portion of the inheritance. He would be appointed as judge over the family, and the father would pray a blessing over him. Jacob thought this was unfair because they were twins. Esau was born only a few seconds before Jacob. This is what created the tension between the two brothers.

As young men, one day Esau had been out hunting, and Jacob was at home cooking.

Genesis 25:29–31 starts the story, "Once when Jacob was cooking some stew, Esau came in from the open country, famished. He said to Jacob, 'Quick, let me have some of that red stew! I'm famished!' Jacob replied, 'First sell me your birthright.'" This is where the story becomes so strange. Who in their right mind would even consider such an offer? Who would trade their inheritance, their future wealth, their future power, and their future blessings for a lousy bowl of stew? Esau made a dumb decision! And, we see this kind of insanity all the time. Highly-intelligent, well-respected, influential leaders destroy their lives because of a ridiculous trade. They trade something incredibly valuable for something of little value.

For instance, some parents who have children (who are of great value), never show up at their football games, school functions, or awards ceremonies. All the missed opportunities because they traded it for a lousy bowl of stew. The stew might be a bottle of alcohol, some pills, a career, a habit, or a hobby containing little lasting value. It leaves kids wondering why their parents couldn't make their game, or why they're getting divorced, or why they can't simply make time for the family. The answer is always the same—they traded their family for a lousy bowl of stew. Millions of people are wounded, damaged, and hurt because they did not manage their appetite.

As we continue the story, Esau says in verse 32 of Genesis chapter 25, "Look, I am about to die. What good is the birthright to me?"

He was about to die? That's quite an exaggeration. He walked in from hunting under his own power. He's weary, tired, and extremely hungry but he wasn't about to die. At this moment, Esau was being driven by an insatiable appetite. A person's desire says, "I have to have that. I need it so bad, I want it, I crave it, I desire it." Be careful. An appetite creates tunnel vision to the point that we see nothing but the object of desire in front of us.

Does this sound familiar? One more drink, one more bite, one more hour at work, one more party, one more website, one more look, one more inappropriate text, or one more fling. The deception is the belief that we can do it one more time, and we'll be satisfied. But there are never enough touchdowns, awards, money, women, thrills, or fame. It will always leave us hungry for more.

Have you noticed how an appetite grows? When you dwell on a desire and feed the appetite, it doesn't shrink but grows.

Here's a true saying: "What you feed will succeed."

Understand why we are easily overcome by what seems to be an uncontrollable desire. At the moment of attraction, our bodies release a pleasure chemical in our brain, causing an intense craving for a euphoric moment. All rational thinking goes out the window, and our focus narrows tightly on the object of desire. We are so focused on the pleasure it's going to bring, we lose sight of any consequences. But, science also reveals that this pleasure chemical flowing through your brain only lasts approximately seven minutes. Impulsive actions rarely serve us well. Don't act or react from strong emotions and feelings, but always out of a clear mind.

We continue the story in Genesis 25:34, "Then Jacob gave

Esau some bread and some lentil stew. He ate and drank, and then got up and left."

Have you ever seen someone act irrationally? They make such a foolish decision that it brings shame or enormous pain into their life. This is what happened here. Esau foolishly and carelessly shoved aside the future God had in store for him. Think about this: God wanted Esau to have twelve sons with large families who would become a great nation. God wanted to introduce Himself to Moses as the God of Abraham, Isaac and *Esau*. But instead, God introduced Himself as the God of Abraham, Isaac and *Jacob*.

God wanted to usher in the birth of His son, Jesus, through Esau's lineage. But God never introduced himself by Esau's name. The out-of-control appetite Esau had led him in a direction that was different than what God had planned for him. What God intended for Esau shifted to Jacob.

Matthew 1:1–2 reads, "This is the genealogy of Jesus the Messiah the son of David, the son of Abraham: Abraham was the father of Isaac, Isaac the father of Jacob, Jacob the father of Judah and his brothers." Esau forfeited God's plan for his life. One foolish decision can alter your entire life. Esau's appetite returned, but his future was destroyed. The "bowl of stew" should be a common conversation in our families. We must help our children identify foolish temptations that want to pull them in a wrong direction. It forces each one of us to ask, "Am I willing to exchange an amazing future for something that satisfies for a short moment?" We must ask ourselves what our bowl of stew is. What is the appetite that could slowly entice and pull me in for its deadly kill?

The most common killers of our children's future are the desire for acceptance, power, fame, money, popularity, pornography, or sex. Don't let these things start creeping in unidentified.

Deadly Predator

One of the deadliest predators that seeks out our children is the pornography industry. When I was young, pornography was something generally accessible only in magazines, guarded behind a counter. Later, the internet allowed pornography into our homes through the family computer. Parents need to realize that with the proliferation of personal mobile devices such as smartphones and tablets, pornographic material can be accessed easily.

The availability and use of pornography has become almost ubiquitous among adolescents. Over the past decade there has been a large increase in the pornographic material that is available to both adults and children. Mainstream pornography use has grown common because it is accessible, affordable, and anonymous. Many times these sites are found by accident, while other times certain sites are talked about among elementary and middle school friends.

It is unfair for our young innocent children to be exposed to graphic images that are forever ingrained into their memory. Porn is a perversion of what God created. For instance, a large part of this industry pushes same-sex relationships. Children who haven't even begun to discover their sexuality are being exposed to these images that create confusion. Kids wonder if they are straight or gay. Along with confusion about sexuality itself comes a sexual flame that is lit too early. This creates an insatiable appetite that can never be satisfied.

Sex and pornography can be a more difficult addiction to break than cocaine. Most people who are addicted to porn are exposed to it at an early stage of their sexual development. As parents and grandparents, we must protect our children and their future as much as possible. Pornography wants you, your husband or wife, your son or daughter, your grandchildren, and your in-laws. It doesn't share well, and it doesn't leave easily. It's a cruel master, and seeks more slaves every day. Here are some ideas that can help protect your children from this beast that is chewing away at this young generation.

Collect Devices at Night

A great safeguard is to never allow your kids to have electronics in their rooms after 9 p.m. or whatever you deem is right. Always have them charge their devices in your bedroom. Becoming tired can impair anyone's judgment. Our kids are certainly no exception. Leaving them alone with their mobile devices during the night can be a dangerous combination.

Install Parental Controls

No parent wants to find out that his or her child has been prematurely exposed to extreme sexual content or violence because they were searching the internet for a word they had heard at school, but didn't know what it was.

Kids are curious and constantly exploring and learning, and that is exactly what they should be doing as they grow. The internet is a massive multidimensional encyclopedia for all the questions kids have.

Simply searching for the word "sex" brings up links that can be incredibly disturbing. Questions and curiosities are not the problem. However, the immediate information that is produced from typing in such a basic word can be traumatic or enticing for a child, and can keep pulling him or her back to those sites. When we give our children access to the internet, we have a huge responsibility to protect them. Talk to friends or research internet filters and parental control software that will protect your children by blocking inappropriate material. This is an absolute must if our kids have electronics.

Be Aware of Sleepovers

Sleepovers may not be that innocent if your child is at someone else's home that doesn't have the same rules and standards as you. Another parent may allow them to stay up with Instagram, Snapchat, texting, calling, or exploring dangerous sites. Don't let sleepovers happen unless you talk to the other child's parent and ask them about their rules and supervision around technology. Make your own rules clear, and ask them to be respected while your child is there.

Communicate with other parents to see what issues or

concerns they have. Help each other make rules and expectations about their safety. Uniting together as a group of parents will bring strength to your rules.

Everything is Digitally Permanent

Teach your children there is no such thing as "delete." Here's a good standard: if they wouldn't say it out loud in front of grandparents or parents, don't say it or send it digitally.

Digital safety experts say there is no such thing as privacy or the ability to erase. What you share digitally is permanent. It never goes away and can always be retrieved. If someone texts a photo or something written in anger, it will not be fully deleted. Texts and pictures can be accessed by the phone company, or in some cases, by police and a court order.

Be conscious and aware of what is being shared via a cell phone. This is very important for kids to learn, because impulse control is much less developed in the teenage years.

Check Video Game Systems

One area that kids and teens are being exposed to sexual content is through gaming networks, which typically have lower privacy settings.

People pose as younger kids or teens, and they can engage in a sexual conversation through a headset or by typing. Make sure kids know that if anyone asks to meet them, they should immediately turn off the device and tell a parent right away.

Be sure they understand the importance of never giving out any personal information like an address, phone, birthday, full name, or location. It's sad that something as innocent as playing a game in your own home can become so dangerous. We live in dangerous times and cannot procrastinate when it comes to protecting our children from being enticed into immoral or sinful actions. Sin always comes back to bite, and the bite is severe!

Living among the Grizzlies

One night, I was watching David Letterman's late night television show. The guest that night was Timothy Treadwell, better known as the Grizzly Man.

He was an American bear-enthusiast, environmentalist, documentary filmmaker, and founder of the bear-protection organization, Grizzly People. He had lived among grizzly bears of Katmai National Park in Alaska for thirteen summers.

He had captured amazing video of himself sitting among the bears and their cubs. That night, as I watched him having close encounters with these predators, I was amazed.

As he sat in the tall grass, a male grizzly walked up to him sniffing and growing. Treadwell would imitate the bears actions by sniffing and growling back. Amazingly, the bear turned and walked away. He would sit with them, touch them, and play with their cubs, knowing that these are among the most dangerous animals on earth. But, he told Letterman he was in no danger because the bears had accepted him as one of their own.

I could feel my heart beating fast and my adrenaline flowing. This was one of the most exhilarating and terrifying things I have ever watched. Letterman was so intrigued by this man, that at the end of the interview he said he'd love to have him back if he weren't eaten first! They were both laughing as the show went to a commercial. I turned off the television thinking about Treadwell and wondering how someone can become so comfortable with something so dangerous.

Repeatedly park rangers and the National Park Service warned Treadwell that his relationship with the bears would inevitably turn deadly. What they feared took place on the afternoon of October 6, 2003. Treadwell and his girlfriend had called in an air taxi by satellite phone, preparing to go home from their summer adventure. The pilot of the small plane circled several times, but could not locate them. Something didn't seem right. He decided to land the aircraft and investigate their camp. When their pilot arrived at their campsite, it seemed abandoned. Then, the pilot noticed a bear in the distance seemingly agitated and protecting his prey.

Looking closer through binoculars, the pilot realized what the bear was protecting were the carcasses of Treadwell and his girlfriend. The pilot said it was the most horrific scene you could ever imagine. The story reminds us that you should never become friendly with a predator. Grizzly bears can stand up to ten feet tall and weigh over seventeen hundred pounds. A grizzly bear is a predator. A predator will always do what a predator does—kill!

The largest and most fierce predator we will ever face is our enemy called the devil. Jesus said that the devil is our enemy who focuses on coming to steal, kill, and destroy.

Think about Treadwell for a moment. He allowed himself to become comfortable, careless, and cozy with something that had the potential of destroying him. In the same way when we take on a pet sin and become comfortable, careless, or cozy with it, we are setting ourselves up to be devoured by the very thing we created an appetite for. We must reinforce to our children to be overly cautious on what kind of appetites we develop. Think of this twist on a well-known saying:

> *Appetites will take you farther than you want to go, keep you longer than you want to stay and cost you more than you want to pay.*

Every action produces a result. Every action leads you somewhere. I like to think of it like this, "Thoughts are like trains, they always take you somewhere." Thoughts are important and must be controlled because thoughts lead to actions, and our actions determine our success or failure in life. I love this saying, "Purity forms our character and our character is the foundation of our destiny." Your destiny cannot outreach your level of character.

Solomon once wrote these words in Proverbs 27:20, "Death and destruction are never satisfied, and neither are human eyes." Solomon had everything the world could offer, but basically he was telling us that our fleshly appetites are never satisfied.

Prisoner of His Own Appetite

In the 4th Century, Duke Edward in Belgium had a severe dispute with his brother Raynald over the affairs of the kingdom. Raynald was grossly overweight and was commonly called by his Latin nickname, Crassus, which means "fat."

After a violent quarrel, Edward led a successful revolt against Raynald. He captured Raynald, but did not kill him. Instead, he built a room around Raynald in the Nieuwkerk castle and promised him he could regain his title and property as soon as he could leave the room. This would not have been difficult for most people, since the room had several windows and a doorway with no door. The servants freely came and went through the opening.

The problem for Raynald was his size prohibited him from fitting through the doorway. To regain his freedom, he needed to lose weight, but Edward knew his older brother's weakness. Each day he sent his brother a variety of delicious foods. Instead of dieting his way out of prison, Raynald grew larger. When Duke Edward was accused of cruelty, he had an answer, "My brother is not a prisoner. He may leave when he so wills." Raynald stayed in that room for the next ten years, until he died. He was a prisoner of his own appetite. He died in bondage because he could not control his hunger.

As we raise our children, relate these stories to them so that they understand they will develop great appetites for certain things in life, but they must determine what they hunger for. Hunger will eventually destroy them or hunger will elevate them. We must teach our children to control their appetites and live with integrity!

CHAPTER 10

Characteristic 4 – Courage

Our youngest son's birth took us by surprise. Brandon came into this world a month early. When we brought him home the day after he was born he was just over four pounds, a tiny beautiful little boy. Growing up, he was always the smallest of his peers and my dad nicknamed him, "Mouse," and that name stuck.

From a very young age, Brandon was athletic and wanted to play soccer, baseball, wrestling, basketball and football. He was extremely talented, but by being so much smaller than all his teammates, he struggled competing with them.

The first year he played football, we went to pick up his uniform and equipment. Part of the process was to weigh all the players. Brandon weighed below the required weight limit. I reluctantly signed the waver giving my permission for him to play. I was hoping I was doing the right thing, as the last thing I wanted was for him to get hurt. They gave him the smallest uniform they had, but it was still too large. When he put on his football pants, they were so big that the knee pads were hanging down between his knees and ankles. I had to pull the pads up to his knee and tape them in place. His shoulder pads were too big, and his helmet wobbled on his head. During the season, each time he ran out on the field all the moms on the sidelines would let out a "Awww, look how little he is!" He didn't take that as a compliment. Brandon found himself very frustrated, standing on the sidelines instead of playing in the game. I remember one game when he stood on the sideline for most of the first half, when the coach finally called his name to go in. I could tell by his body language and the way he ran out on the field, there was not an ounce of fear or intimidation in him. He was on the field ready to make a statement. A couple of plays later the other team pitched the ball to their running back, heading right in Brandon's direction. Brandon was running at full speed as he set his sights on the running back coming in his direction. Brandon hit him with all his might. The force of the hit knocked the running back completely off his feet and into the sidelines. The coaches and team went crazy. The hardest hit of the season came from the most unlikely source.

From that moment, everything changed. Instead of standing on the sidelines, he was playing in the game. He was small, but the coaches saw that he had courage, and he became recognized as one of the best players on the team. My mom and dad were in town that weekend and after that game my dad changed his nickname from "Mouse" to "Mighty Mouse."

Heroes

Superhero movies always seem to be blockbusters, and for good reason. We admire the courage of those willing to save others as well as the world. Who doesn't want to be a hero?

Our love for heroes is why we are so drawn to stories such as a shepherd boy named David facing a giant named Goliath, or Gilgamesh defeating the monster Humbaba, or Harry Potter and his friends confronting deadly Lord Voldemort. There's something exhilarating about courageous individuals, pitted against the odds, rising above fear, and showing little concern for their own safety.

Where does courage come from, and why are some naturally braver and daring than others? When I think about extreme risk-taking activities, they defy common sense and logic. People are willingly desiring to take part in activities like sky-diving, paragliding, diving with sharks, or bungee jumping off a bridge? Events like these can create high levels of stress for most, yet a small group of "thrill seekers" will experience moments of ecstasy that keeps them coming back again and again, like addicts.

In the risk taker's brain, science reveals that there are fewer dopamine-inhibiting receptors, meaning that their brains are more saturated with the dopamine chemical, predisposing them to taking risks or chasing the next high. We look at thrill seekers, wondering where this kind of courage comes from. I am not naturally drawn to thrill-seeking activities, but I do have a strong desire to be strong and courageous in my day-to-day life.

Courage is the ability to do something difficult even when there's risk. Courageous people do and say what they think is right, despite opposition. Without courage, you'll never take action toward your hopes and dreams. It's the grit needed to overcome your fears and weaknesses. It's the same grit needed to take risk. Courage says, "I am not yet what I can be, and I can do something about it." Having dreams of what our lives can be without courage is self-sabotaging. Nothing worthwhile happens without the mixture of hard work and courage.

Brandon's courageous spirit was developed at a young age, which became a trait that has followed him into adulthood. It's important to help establish courage in our children when they are young. When Brandon graduated from his university with a major in theology, we wanted to bring him back to our church to lead our young adult and college ministry. It was a well-established ministry with about one hundred and fifty students attending.

Coming out of college, Brandon had very little experience speaking in front of people. Turning over this size of ministry to him was risky. I'll never forget Dustin, his older brother, and I sitting in the auditorium to hear his first sermon.

He finished preaching, and I turned to Dustin and said, "This is not going to work, he's too inexperienced. He's not ready for this size of ministry." When Brandon walked off the stage, he knew it was rough. He felt incredibly insecure trying to fill the shoes of his older brother who had built a successful college ministry. Later, in a meeting about his future and his role as the leader of our college ministry, I saw the same body language and facial expression I had seen in him years ago playing football. Instead of cowering under the pressure of being inexperienced, he totally committed himself to succeeding. In all my years of ministry, I have never seen anyone grow and advance themselves in talent and ability as fast as Brandon did. He studied world-class speakers. He studied comedians and their timing in making people laugh. He read from great preachers and scholars of our past. He became a student of God's Word. Each week he watched and analyzed his own sermons.

Through a courageous spirit, he rapidly began to advance. People began to take notice, and now he's recognized as leading one of the largest college and young adult ministries in the nation. Today he is being asked to speak at different functions around the world. When I reflect on his story, I realize courage is the formula of transforming you from a "Mouse" to "Mighty Mouse."

> *The character trait of courage is a must for every world changer.*

World changers are action-driven, and they act on their passion, purpose and dreams. Merely talking about their dreams is never enough. John F. Kennedy, the 35th president of the United States, said, "There are risks and costs to action but they are far less than the long-range risks of comfortable inaction."

The first South African black president who set South

Africans free from the atrocities of apartheid, Dr. Nelson Mandela, changed the world through his influence and leadership, and we have an international day every July 18 that celebrates his determination and commitment to seeing everyone as equal.

Mandela stated,

> During my lifetime, I have dedicated myself to this struggle of the African people. I have fought against white domination, and I have fought against black domination. I have cherished the ideal of a democratic and free society in which all persons live together in harmony and with equal opportunities. It is an ideal which I hope to live for and to achieve. But if need be, it is an ideal for which I am prepared to die.

Mandela went to prison for twenty-seven years for this ideal and today there is a democratic society that he once only saw in his imagination. That's a man of courage.

Grit may come from our own human drive, but true courage comes from a much deeper source, our faith in God.

As you tell your children stories of courage, don't forget to tell them one of the most important stories of all, the ones recorded in the Bible. David and Goliath is not a simple childhood story, but a true account of what it means to have courage in the face of the worst possible circumstances.

The Story of David and Goliath

Three thousand years ago, in the Valley of Elah, a massive man named Goliath of Gath stepped out of the Philistine ranks to defy and taunt the army of Israel and its God. For forty days, he harangued the Israelite warriors, heaping shame on them, since none dared to accept his fight-to-the-death, winner-takes-all challenge. Every morning when he stepped forward, the men of Israel shrank back. Then, a teenage shepherd boy named David showed up in the camp with some bread and cheese for his brothers, and heard the giant pour out his scorn on the people of his Lord. David was indignant. So, he took his shepherd's sling, grabbed a few stones, hit Goliath in the forehead, and chopped off his head.

Many think David's defeat of Goliath is a story of personal courage in the face of overwhelming odds, or having the raw courage to stand up to an arrogant, powerful giant. We wish we could have just a small amount of the courage David had, but that's a misconception. It's true that he was courageous, and courage is a glorious virtue. But, David's courage was a derivative virtue.

Before looking at where David's courage came from, we need to ask why Saul and his soldiers lacked it. At first, it seems obvious. The Philistine champion was about nine-feet-tall and incredibly strong. He was a highly trained, experienced, killing machine. Physically, every man in the Hebrew camp was outclassed. Fighting Goliath looked like suicide. At this moment, for whatever reason, despite all the stories and past experiences they had with God, Goliath looked bigger than God. Each man believed that if he went out against this enormous human, they would be destroyed.

David's Courage Came from God

So, what made David different? It was not because he had the self-generated, raw, cool courage of an American action-movie hero. What fueled David's courage was his trust in God's promises and God's power to fulfill them. Years before, Samuel, the prophet, had informed David that God had chosen him to be the next king of Israel and anointed him. David knew this information when he arrived in the camp and heard Goliath's sneering rants. And, he drew additional confidence by remembering how God had helped him in the past.

> *He was not courageous on his own, but he was courageous because he believed in God.*

David believed that God would never break His promise. If Goliath made himself an obstacle to God's promise, God would take care of David. David saw God as bigger and stronger than the giant Philistine. So, he went out to fight knowing that God would give him victory over Goliath and when he did, the victory would demonstrate God's power and faithfulness.

Courage is not an autonomous or a self-generated virtue. Courage is always produced by faith. For the Christian, a lack of courage, or what the writer of Hebrews calls, "shrinking back"

(Hebrews 10:37–38), is always evidence of a lack of faith in a promise of God. When we allow a "Goliath" to be larger than our God, we see how weak and inadequate we are to face him. Fighting him seems impossible, and the thought immobilizes us. All of us experience this kind of fear. David did too. He is such a helpful example for us because he so frequently felt fearful, and needed to encourage himself repeatedly, as shown in his writings in the Psalms.

A New Kind of Giant-Slaying

David battled a physical enemy. In the New Testament, we are not to battle flesh and blood (Ephesians 6:12). Our "Goliaths" are our indwelling sins and the "spiritual forces of wickedness that come against us." We are to pick up our weapons of spiritual warfare including the shield of faith and the sword of God's Word. Our courage to face wickedness will not come from our self-confidence, it will only come from confidence in God's powerful promises.

Whatever situation you or your children are facing, here are several steps to help build up courage:

- Thank the Lord daily for always being with you, and even having you engraved on the palms of His hands (Isaiah 49:16).
- Encourage yourself that you can do all things through Him because He will be your strength (Philippians 4:13).

- The Lord has promised that He will strengthen and help you, and uphold you with the right hand of His righteousness (Isaiah 41:10).

- Be comforted by the fact that Jesus battled all the same temptations, fears, and dangers that you are going through. He is filled with compassion for your pain and struggles, and can help you (Hebrews 2:18).

- Don't try to manufacture courage in your own strength. When you are weak, then He is strong! Encourage yourself out loud with the words: "Let the weakling say, 'I am strong'" (Joel 3:10).

- Recite Psalm 91 out loud. The secret to building courage is in the first line, "Whoever dwells in the shelter of the Most High will rest in the shadow of the Almighty."

- Open the Word daily and meditate on it. Personalize Psalm 91 by inserting "me" in every line where it's appropriate, such as, "Surely He will save me." I guarantee that soon you will find faith building up inside, and courage flowing out!

Children and teens are growing up in a world that is becoming increasingly competitive and comparative. It is easy for them, or for us, to believe that the ones who have found success or happiness are better, stronger, smarter, or luckier than we are. The truth is that none of us are born with the "success" gene or the "happiness" gene. There are many things that lead to success and happiness, but one of the most powerful of these is courage. When we run straight into failures, rejections, and unexpected turns, courage allows us to keep going, to find a different way, and to try again.

Explain to Your Kids What Courage Really Is

For kids and teens, one of the most important things for them to know is that courage doesn't always feel like courage. From the outside, courage often looks impressive and powerful and self-assured. Sometimes it might look reckless or thrilling. From the inside, though, it can feel frightening and unpredictable. It can feel like anxiety, or fear, or self-doubt. It often looks different from the outside to the way you expect it to feel on the inside.

This is because courage and fear always exist together.

It can't be any other way. If there is no fear, there is no need for courage. Courage isn't something magical that happens inside us to keep us from being scared. It's about something that happens inside us to make us push through fear, self-doubt, and anxiety. It helps us do the things that feel hard, or risky, or frightening. Speak to the courage you already see in your kids. Kids and teens step up to expectations set before them. Speak to the courage that is coming to life inside them as though it's already there:

- I know how brave you are.
- I love that you made a hard decision, even when it would be easier to do the other thing.
- You might not feel brave, but you are one of the bravest people I know.

These kinds of comments are exactly what your future world influencer needs to hear from you. Also, remind them that failure and rejection can be a sign of them attempting something that requires courage. Every new experience gives them new information and new wisdom that they wouldn't have otherwise. This is the reason only the brave reach high levels of success. It's so important to constantly encourage kids to do activities that push them to the edges of their physical or emotional selves, such as drama, sports, or music. Encourage anything that will help nurture the truth that they are strong, powerful, and can cope with anything they face.

You are Their Example of Courage

Everything you do is gold in their eyes. Talk to them about the times you feel nervous, or the times you've said, "No," or "Yes," when everyone else was moving in the opposite direction. Talk to them about the times you've pushed through fear, exhaustion, sadness, or anger to do the right thing. Talk about the times you took risks, even when you were afraid. Let them feel that the courage in you is also in them.

Sometimes courage is about doing a scary thing, and

sometimes it's about doing the right thing. Sometimes saying, "No," to someone, or something that doesn't feel right, is one of the bravest things they can do. There are three questions they can ask themselves that will help them wade through all the noise, and find the right thing to do when faced with negative peer pressure:

- Will it hurt someone?
- Will my parents and God approve of this action?
- Will it break an important rule or is it against the law?

Deciding whether something is right or wrong is the first step. The next part is the hard part, which is finding a way out. It's not always easy saying "No," which is why courage is needed. Give children some options to try. These might involve leaving and going home, suggesting something else to do instead, or making a joke, "Nope, there's no way I'm getting myself into trouble today, out of all the ways to get grounded, that's not worth the trouble."

Our kids might believe that courage is the grand action of a dragon-slayer, but the truth is, our children are slaying their own dragons every day. It's important for them to see themselves as strong and able to push through, even when they feel small, scared, confused, or unseen.

Emma Donoghue, having been abducted and trapped for years, stated it best in her book *Room*, "Scared is what you're feeling. Brave is what you're doing." Be the example of courage your children need.

CHAPTER 11

Characteristic 5 – Vision

When our three boys were young, our oldest son, Dustin, and our youngest son, Brandon, were incredibly athletic. Both boys had natural athletic abilities that came very easily for them. Jonathan, our middle son, was not born with those same natural athletic abilities. As a young boy, he could not throw a ball well at all. He had a very awkward throwing motion, and it frustrated him horribly when we would play catch in the backyard.

While Dustin and Brandon were convinced that they would be professional athletes playing baseball for the Atlanta Braves or football for the Dallas Cowboys, Jonathan did not share those aspirations. Jonathan excelled in academics and found it easy to be content playing video games in his room all day. I knew that wasn't healthy and he needed to be more socially engaged and physically active. I found it challenging trying to find the delicate balance between encouraging him to pursue something he couldn't see was worthwhile, or pushing too hard to play in a competitive sport.

It's always positive to get your kids to do things that are challenging, because it helps them develop grit and flexibility. It also provides a vision of a positive future. For a parent, it takes common sense and wisdom to know how much pressure to apply. For Jonathan, the gentle pushing to play sports kept him healthy, strong, and improved his agility and his social interaction. The most important thing was giving him the latitude to play the sport that best suited him, instead of dictating the sport I wanted him to play. But, I knew I had to create a vision for Jonathan, a vision of what he could achieve.

Proverbs 12:18 states, "The words of the reckless pierce like swords, but the tongue of the wise brings healing." The Bible clearly tells us that if we look to find our own way, then we are a fool. We are to find advice from those who are wiser than we are. It is the only way we can develop as people and as visionary leaders.

Who are Visionary Leaders?

Visionary leaders are the builders of a new dawn, working with imagination, insight, and boldness. They present a challenge that calls forth the best in people, and brings them together around a shared sense of purpose. Their eyes are on the horizon, and not on what is near at hand. They are innovators and change agents, seeing the big picture and thinking strategically. Visionaries have the unique ability to see life and situations from a thirty-thousand-foot view which helps them make course corrections and avoid problems others do not see.

They search for solutions that transcend common approaches, and find answers that address multiple sides of an issue to create real breakthroughs.

Repeatedly, I have emphasized the importance of teaching your children through the principle of storytelling. The characteristic of vision is perhaps the most important one of all for your children to learn, as it will strengthen their determination so they can change their world.

The Story of Nehemiah

In 444 B.C., Nehemiah worked for the King of Persia as a cupbearer. He tasted the wine and food before the king to make sure that no one had tried to poison the king. However, Nehemiah became much more than a cupbearer. He found favor with the king and became his friend, even though he was a Jewish slave.

One hundred years before Nehemiah's time, the Babylonians had conquered Israel, destroyed their temple, and torn down the walls that surrounded Jerusalem. Nebuchadnezzar captured many of the Israelites as slaves. Among those captured were Shadrach, Meshach, Abednego, and Daniel. Ten decades later, Nehemiah is a descendant of the Jews who is working for the king. He heard reports about Jewish people still living in the rubble of the destroyed city. The news of their suffering and extreme poverty was heartbreaking to him. His heart was heavy for his homeland and his people, so he decided to do something extremely risky. He asked the king for permission to go back to Jerusalem and rebuild its walls. Nehemiah wasn't an employee of the king; he was a slave. Slaves don't get time off. But, Nehemiah had proven himself as loyal and faithful, so the king gave him permission to rebuild Jerusalem's walls. The king made him the governor of Jerusalem. The people living in Jerusalem had only lived in a city of rubble and poverty. They were a poor, defeated people, surrounded by strong warlords that would steal from them regularly.

When Nehemiah arrived in Jerusalem, he spent a whole day touring the city and assessing the damage. What he saw was discouraging. At that moment, he concluded that if he didn't get anything else done in his life, he was going to rebuild Jerusalem's walls. Problems were everywhere, but the most important one to tackle was the rebuilding of the walls to provide his people protection. He called together all the people who lived in the city and surrounding region to cast an unbelievably compelling vision. Nehemiah cast the vision to rebuild the city walls with clarity, by inspiring the Jewish people to see the full scope of the problem and to envision the solution.

Here are the five things Nehemiah did to cast the vision:

- he explained the problem
- he provided the solution
- he explained why it was important
- he told how it would work
- he told them they had to start now

The Jewish people heard Nehemiah speak with such passion, they rallied together and began to rebuild the wall around the city. However, the building process had hardly begun when the enemies of Israel realized that a wall would allow Israel to grow in strength again.

Sanballat was a person who led the opposition to stop the wall from being built. He tried to distract Nehemiah from the work and even lure him outside the city to kill him. Nehemiah 6:1–2, "When word came to Sanballat, Tobiah, Gesham the Arab and the rest of our enemies that I had rebuilt the wall and not a gap was left in it…[they] sent me this message: 'Come, let us meet together…' But they were scheming to harm me." The enemies realized they could not stop the wall unless they stopped Nehemiah and got him down from his ladder.

They were trying to entice Nehemiah to have lunch, or breakfast, or maybe coffee. But, Nehemiah knew they wanted to kill him. Nehemiah 6:3, "So I sent messengers to them with this reply, 'I am carrying on a great project and cannot go down. Why should the work stop while I leave it and go down to you?'" Nehemiah was doing a great work and could not come down. This may be one of the greatest statements in the Bible. In other words, Nehemiah had a vision and a plan, and nothing was going to distract him from it.

> *Visionary leaders recognize the important task at hand, and push away any distractions.*

Nehemiah's enemies didn't give up. Four times they sent messages requesting him to come down off the ladder, and Nehemiah answered them the same every time.

When your kids become discouraged, defeated, tired, or

intimidated, remind them, "Don't get distracted. Keep your focus on seeing your vision come to fulfillment. Your dream can be killed by a simple distraction. Continue the work until it is accomplished."

I love thinking back on my earlier story about my boys and their athletic endeavors, because out of all three boys, only one of them went on to became a NCAA Division I college athlete. I will never forget sitting in an indoor stadium watching the NCAA Division I Track and Field competition with some of the best athletes in the country. Some competing that day were Olympic champions holding world records. The atmosphere was electrifying. It was a thrill for us to watch our son compete at this world class level. I was a nervous wreck waiting for him to compete, as this was one of the most intense environments I've ever been in.

What made the situation even more exciting for me was *which* son I was watching. It was the one who had few natural athletic abilities and little natural agility. Jonathan had become a Division I pole vaulter. The vision that was planted in him when he was young was coming to fruition. This is a great reminder for us as parents as well as for our kids.

What's Your Broken Wall?

You might be struggling in your marriage and you know if something doesn't change, it has the potential to damage the entire family. A struggling marriage is like a broken-down wall. The enemy seeks out and finds the weakness in your fortress and is relentless in his attacks. If this is the case, get on the ladder and don't come down until your marriage is fully repaired. Every time you look at the picture of your spouse that's sitting on your desk or on your phone, say to yourself, "I'm doing a great work, I could work more hours, I could make more money, I could go on more business trips, but I choose to get on the ladder and restore my marriage. I'm not coming down until all is restored."

Some people have health challenges. They're too sedentary, battling diabetes by being overweight, eating unhealthily, or not exercising. Walking up a flight of stairs causes shortness of breath. But know this: God gave us our bodies to fulfill our God-given purpose. Others can't be helped when we're suffering from self-inflicted unhealthiness. Get on the ladder today and don't come down until health is restored. Say to yourself, "I'm doing a great work and I can't come down until I'm finished."

Some people need to rebuild the wall with their children. Don't get distracted. Build the wall. Stay focused. When we look at our children, we need to see them as great work. There are a lot of things that can take up our time. It's easy to be busy, but our kids are more important, and we must live that out. We are not coming down. When kids are teenagers, we look at their bodies and wonder how they got so big, so fast. We need to remind ourselves that this is our great work, and we're not going to get distracted. Then we'll have the great privilege of watching them grow up and accomplish more than we ever imagined. That's a visionary parent leader.

> *Don't get off the ladder.*

Say out loud, "I'm doing a great work and I can't come down until I'm finished."

For those who are teenagers, college students, or young single adults, you are at the most critical stage of life. The biggest life decisions typically are made at this stage. Your friends will shape your world view. Your habits will most likely follow you the rest of your life. The people you date and eventually marry will greatly determine your life. At this stage of life, your spiritual foundation is formed. You have the choice to feed it or let it die.

> *Seeking out a meaningful and transformational relationship with Christ will be the most important thing you can do, because Christ will become the central focus of your life.*

In this age bracket, you are part of the most informed generation that has ever lived. There are significant numbers of visionaries rising from your generation. If you are part of this generation, identify any breaks or weaknesses in your own personal wall. Discover what sets you up for disaster, and what sets you up for success. Have a vision for your future, climb the ladder, start working, and don't come down until you've achieved your goal. This is exactly what we see in Nehemiah's story.

Nehemiah 6:15 states, "So the wall was completed…in fifty-two days." It was quite an accomplishment to rebuild a wall in fifty-two days that had been laying in rubble for over one hundred years. Verse 16 continues, "When all our enemies heard about this, all the surrounding nations were afraid and lost their self-confidence; because they realized that this work had been done with the help of our God."

Developing Visionaries

In an earlier chapter, I mentioned we were landscaping our backyard when our boys were in high school. We were doing it ourselves and it was a gigantic job. We poured sidewalks, laid sod, and moved tons of landscaping rock with wheelbarrows.

During that summer, I told Dustin that instead of getting a summer job, I would pay him to landscape the backyard. I was very clear how I wanted everything done. His main job was hauling rock in a wheelbarrow and spreading it over a very large area. After he had been working for a few days, I came home for lunch to see how he coming along. I walked in the door to find Dustin sitting on the couch with no shirt on, drinking iced tea. I said to him, "I thought I was paying you to work in the backyard." Without a word, he pointed toward the window. I walked over, and saw four of his friends hauling the rock and spreading it out, while he was watching television in the air-conditioned house. I was frustrated because I was paying him to do a job and not just sit the couch. I told him, "Dustin, I don't have enough money to pay all your friends to do what I hired you to do."

He responded, "Don't worry about it, it's all taken care of. My friends wanted to hang out and do something today, so I told them if they came and helped me for two hours, I would take them out for their favorite pizza. Four friends working two hours each is a total of eight hours of work. I can buy them pizza, hang out, have fun, and still have money left over." I walked out the door to go back to work still frustrated, but as I was driving back to the church, I found myself laughing at what I had witnessed. It was brilliant!

It's in moments like these that we can see the beginning of leadership traits starting to sprout. We can't get frustrated by it, but need to be quick to encourage and develop it. It's pushing and guiding our kids to think with a vision. We must teach them to see beyond circumstances, and inspire others to rally around a cause. This is the formation of them becoming a visionary leader. As our children grow, the simple life lessons we teach them will become more sophisticated over time. One of the most important lessons is how to communicate and collaborate with other people, especially in school and eventually at work, because that will increase their effectiveness and success in life.

Great leaders are people who develop great leaders, and great visionary leader parents develop their children into great future leaders. Here's something to keep in mind: if we, as parents, aren't being mentored, then how can we mentor our children effectively. True mentors are continually learning. For instance, when you go to church, don't go simply to fulfill an obligation. Arrive early and find a seat close to the front. Carry a journal with you to take notes. Write down thoughts, phrases, principles, and Bible verses. Reflect on your notes many times throughout the week. Instead of simply hearing a sermon, begin a method of spiritual growth that will enhance every aspect of your life.

Find a Bible study or small group to attend with friends. Meet someone with more knowledge and experience for coffee. To effectively lead children, a parent must position him or herself as a learner. Push yourself to be a visionary. A commitment to strong biblical values becomes the compass to move us in the right direction.

> *Values that set a solid foundation for life come from the Word of God, which is an unshakeable standard.*

Visionaries are self-aware and reflective. Visionary leaders follow an inner sense of direction from the Holy Spirit and lead from the inside out. Rather than allowing power to corrupt them, visionary leaders are elevated by the power of spiritual moral leadership to bring life to others. Visionary leadership is based on a balanced expression of the spiritual, mental, emotional, and physical dimensions. It requires core values, clear vision, empowering relationships, and innovative action. Here are eight traits found in visionary leaders that will help us to develop this trait within our children.

Inspirational

What does being inspirational mean? Visionary leaders tap into our emotions. They ignite passions in people to accomplish tasks that change the course of human life.

Emotionally Intelligent

Visionary leaders have the capacity to be aware of, control, and express their emotions, and to handle interpersonal relationships. Emotional intelligence is the key to both personal and professional success.

A leader must be aware of his or her emotions and be empathetic to the feelings of others. Only through empathy can a leader connect with the hearts of their team, and inspire them to realize their greatness.

Imaginative

Visionary leaders have a childlike playfulness. They value their imagination and allow themselves to dream, exercising their mind's eye to see beyond what's in the physical world. They encourage others to dream big, too.

Resolute

Social pressures influence visionary leaders less than others. Their high convictions hold strong in the face of adversity. Setbacks aren't a sign of failure to them; they are mere stopping points on the way to realizing their vision.

Collaborative

A vision cannot be accomplished alone. It takes a team to do it together. Visionary leaders inspire others to harness their unique gifts and strengths to innovate and find creative solutions. They create an open environment where people learn to trust each other.

Bold

There's no place for timidity in visionary leadership. These leaders are courageous and daring, willing to take calculated risks. They don't fear failure as much as they fear not trying.

Magnetic

Visionary leaders are inclusive, inviting others to make the vision their own. They attract talented people who are passionate about what they do and are inspired by the big picture.

They create thriving, innovative cultures where individuals have the freedom to create their best work and take pride in their efforts. Visionary leaders bring out the best in people.

Optimistic

Visionary leaders hold a positive outlook for the future. They are hopeful for success. They don't view problems as personal or permanent. They view them as obstacles. Their optimism is a sturdy anchor when setbacks occur.

Although this visionary leadership style may come more naturally to some, it's a style of leading that can be learned. It's a set pattern of behavior that we can purposely encode within our minds.

Alexander the Great

Known as the "Man Who Conquered the World," Alexander the Great is regarded as one of the greatest military leaders of all time. Born in 356 B.C., he created the largest empire in history, stretching from Greece to India, by the time he was thirty-three years old. During his reign, he did a lot of noble deeds, including one that unified the Greek city-states. While he was undefeated in battle, he succumbed to malaria and died in 323 B.C. As a visionary leader, his greatest qualities were his vision, foresight and military capabilities.

As the world changes each day, we will see children being born and people dying, yet life continues. In the mundane things of life, people will be born with a different ability and flair to influence others. When we talk about people who are "visionaries," we speak with an undertone of reverence, as though they possess a natural gift. But, the clear majority of visionary leaders are cultivated over time, just as a book may take months or even years to write.

Visionaries are people who add the trait of forward-thinking to their way of life. The best way to teach this trait to our children is to first establish it into our own life. They learn by seeing, and will begin to mimic the actions of forward thinking to become a visionary leader.

SECTION 4

Time to Build Your Legacy

These five characteristics are seemingly simple: Confidence, Honor, Integrity, Courage, and Vision. These five characteristics can be poured into our children by telling and re-telling the biblical stories of people who have encountered God, allowing our children to not be influenced by the world, but to be the influence for their friends and family. As we shape and guide our children with these characteristics each day, we are leaving a legacy through them to change the world.

CHAPTER 12

Leaving a Legacy

In December 1974, Harry Chapin released a song, *The Cat's in the Cradle*. It hit number one on the pop charts and was inducted into the Grammy Hall of Fame in 2011. Throughout the song, while his boy is growing up, a busy father makes excuses for not spending quality time with him. Eventually, the son grows up and the shoe is on the other foot. The grown son doesn't have time for his elderly father. As the song concludes, the father laments that his son had grown up to be just like himself. I think it's the most gut-wrenching song I've ever heard. It makes us shudder to think we might end up with that kind of regret. This song resonated with so many people because of the absent father problem in our society.

Do you ever find yourself looking at your teenage kids and feel a tinge of sadness that you didn't make more of the time you had together while they were still young? If so, you're not alone. Many parents have a long list of regrets.

According to a national survey, here are some of the top regrets of parents:

- working too much
- worrying too much about little things that didn't really matter
- not playing with kids more
- not going on more vacations
- not taking enough photos
- spending too much time away from kids
- not reading enough to kids at bedtime
- spending too much time worrying about keeping the house clean
- not being at milestones in kids' lives
- being too overprotective

I don't think there is a parent alive that doesn't look back with regret, and for the most part that's normal. We often look back and think, "I could have done that better." Now with grown children, the new chapter of our life is to watch our legacy unfold with our children and grandchildren. With great anticipation, I will watch the generational power of influence and investment flow through our three sons and their wives into their sons and daughters. Legacy is something handed down from one generation to the next. This definition has transitioned to largely refer to the money that someone hands down once they die. However, this word carries a worth greater than any legacy of money.

For a believer, their legacy is their testimony or their story that will be passed down to the next generation and remembered long after they are is gone. It is the emotions that people feel when they hear your name. It's the stories they tell about you as they tuck their children into bed. It's the encouragement they receive during tough days as they remember your example and your words. That's a legacy!

Psalm 145:4 reads, "One generation commends your works to another; they tell of your mighty acts."

There was a family who had a priceless family heirloom, a vase that was passed down from one generation to the next. One day, the family who had it left their teenagers at home while they went out shopping. When they returned home, their children met them at the door with sad faces, reporting, "Mom and Dad, you know that priceless heirloom our family passes down from one generation to the next? Well, our generation just dropped it." Each generation has spiritual memories, experiences, stories, and values it wants to pass along to the next generation. We don't want to be the generation that drops something so valuable.

I have talked to so many fathers that carry guilt and regret because of their absence and lack of investment in their kids' lives. They realize they dropped a priceless family heirloom such as time, love, or care. It is important to remember that history can't be changed, but the future *can* be made into anything you want it to be. Here's a fascinating story from American history that illustrates the difference between our heritage and our legacy.

Edwin Booth died with a letter in his pocket that reminds us of how anybody at anytime can use his or her potential influence to make a difference. At one time, Edwin Booth was considered one of the greatest actors in the world. His career was taking off until a fatal shooting took place in April, 1865. His brother, John Wilkes Booth, had assassinated President Abraham Lincoln.

The stigma of that single act drove Edwin into retirement and seclusion. He knew for the rest of his life that when someone heard the name, "Booth," they would think of John Wilkes Booth. The family name had been forever tainted by his brother's evil deed. However, Edwin Booth's legacy turned out differently than that.

During a busy event in Jersey City, Edwin was standing at the train station near a young man. The young man suddenly lost his footing on the platform and fell onto the tracks as a train was swiftly moving toward him. Without hesitation, Edwin risked his own life to pull this stranger from the tracks below. There was a brief exchange of extreme gratitude between the two, and the young man disappeared in the crowd. Edwin could have never dreamed how significant that one moment would become. Weeks later he received a letter from Ulysses Grant's chief secretary. It was a letter of thanks for his heroic deed, because the life that Edwin Booth saved that day was Robert Todd Lincoln, the son of Abraham Lincoln.

John Wilkes Booth killed Abraham Lincoln bringing shame upon the family. Edwin Booth saved the life of Abraham Lincoln's son and brought honor upon the family. Edwin Booth took Grant's letter to the grave, because it was a reminder:

> *We may not be able to change our heritage, but we can change our legacy.*

Your family history may not have been the best, but the legacy you leave is going to be great!

The Incomplete Handoff

In the 2004 Summer Olympic Games in Athens, Greece, the American women's 4x100 relay team was favored to win the gold medal. The team featured Marion Jones, a sprinter who had won four gold medals at the previous Olympics in Sydney. The American team was already off to a strong start when Jones took the baton for the second leg of the race. She gained ground as she ran her leg and approached Lauryn Williams, a young speedster who would run the third leg.

Williams began running as Jones drew near, but when she reached back to receive the baton, they couldn't seem to complete the handoff. Once, twice, three times, Jones thrust the baton forward, but each time it missed William's hand, or she couldn't seem to wrap her fingers around it. Finally, on the fourth try, they made the connection, but by that time they had crossed out of the twenty-yard exchange zone and were disqualified. Everyone knew they were the fastest team on the track. The night before, they'd had the fastest qualifying time. But, when they couldn't complete the handoff, their race was over.

In track and field, the four-person relay is centered on

successfully passing a baton from one runner to the next. A handoff outside the exchange zone disqualifies the team, and a fumbled baton leaves the team far behind in the race.

The handoff of God's truth to the next generation must also occur during a specific window of time and must not be dropped in the exchange. Kids need to see and hear real faith in their parents' lives. Those who run before set the pace for those who follow.

As important as it is for the previous generation to set the pace by living authentically, at a certain point, a handoff must be made in which the next generation receives the baton of faith and begins to run with it. That handoff isn't as easy as it looks, nor is it automatic. A successful handoff is the result of thousands and thousands of practice runs.

A Generation Who Did Not Know God

Joshua was the man God chose to lead the children of Israel into the Promised Land, and he displayed incredible strength and courage. He was a mighty man of faith and an inspiring leader, but the next generation didn't take the baton successfully.

Judges 2:7–8, 10 reads,

> The people served the Lord throughout the lifetime of Joshua and of the elders who outlived him and who had seen all the great things the Lord had done for Israel. Joshua son of Nun, the

servant of the Lord, died at the age of a hundred
and ten. After that whole generation had been
gathered to their ancestors, another generation
grew up who knew neither the Lord nor what He
had done for Israel.

I find it almost incomprehensible that Joshua and his
generation dropped the baton from one generation to the next.
They had defeated the Amalekites, crossed the Jordan River
on dry ground, and had seen the walls of Jericho come down.
They had seen the sun stand still. Yet after these miracles, the
next generation did not know the Lord or the work he had done
for Israel.

What happened? Where was the legacy of Joshua's
generation? We don't know what happened, but something went
horribly wrong. It had a crippling effect on the next generation.
Whatever the reasons, they dropped the baton of faith.

Every generation has a tremendous responsibility. If we
hand off the baton well to the next generation, then we represent
God as a powerful and loving God. If we hand the baton off
poorly to the next generation, we represent God as small and
meaningless. The baton you carry has the potential to advance
the kingdom of darkness or advance the kingdom of God.

Parents, you're holding the baton, and God has strategically
placed children in your life to receive it. This is a sobering
thought. It should cause each one of us to tremble a little,
realizing that the moment we choose to bring children into
this world, all selfishness must die. Parenthood is sacrificial,

laying down your life that they might live abundantly. That sounds strangely familiar. It sounds like Jesus who came to serve mankind and sacrifice that we might live abundantly. Parenthood must be approached with pinpoint accuracy. There can be no vagueness of what our goal as a parent is. We are raising up an army of God. We cannot assume past faithfulness will continue in our children and their children. Each generation must be taught who God is, and what He has done for mankind.

Could we be in danger of losing an entire generation, as Israel did? The sobering statistics indicate that we are failing to pass on the essential beliefs and values of Christianity. Here are two statistics:

- Of youth from Christian homes attending public schools, 85 percent do not hold a biblical worldview.
- About eight million twenty-somethings who were active churchgoers as teenagers will no longer be active in church by their thirtieth birthdays.

The National Study of Youth and Religion did extensive research on the religious lives of U.S. teenagers:

- Most teenagers are incredibly inarticulate about their faith and its meaning in their lives. They find it almost impossible to put basic beliefs into words.
- Teens are "functional deists," that is, they believe God exists, created the world, and set life in motion, but that He only becomes involved with them personally to make their lives happier or to solve problems.

- Many teens, including conservative Protestants, reject the essential doctrine of salvation by grace; three out of five believe people can earn a place in heaven if they are generally good, or do enough good things for others.
- When deciding right from wrong in difficult situations, only 31 percent of Southern Baptist teens said they turn to God or the Scriptures.

Clearly this means that an enormous amount of self-proclaimed Christian families have passed down no spiritual plan or vision to their children. They are going through the motions by attending church periodically and carrying the label of Christian, but it has no real meaning in their day-to-day life. If God doesn't carry much significance in the parent's life, it will be much less in their children's lives. We pass down what we are passionate about.

I Did It for You, Dad

Bill Havens was on the first team of canoeists scheduled to represent the United States in Paris at the 1924 Summer Olympics. For months, he trained on the Potomac River with the Washington Canoe Club, preparing physically and mentally for the games.

Bill was undefeated in both the one-man single-blade and double-blade events, and had high hopes of bringing home the gold. But, just weeks before the team was set to sail for Paris, Bill was forced to face the reality that his expectant wife was due in late July. This was the exact time at which Bill would be competing on the other side of the world.

The decision, though not easy, was obvious to Bill. He forfeited his spot on the team. His brother, Bud Havens, and the rest of the U.S. canoe crew won three gold, one silver and two bronze medals over six events at the Olympics. Four days later Bill's son, Frank, came into the world. Bill never made it to another Olympics. In 1948, his son, Frank, started training for the 1952 Olympic Games. His coach was none other than his own father Bill.

Frank and his dad spent the better part of the ensuing four years on the water together, training hard. When Frank went to the 1952 Olympic games in Helsinki, he set a new World Record and took home the gold in the solo ten-thousand-meter event.

In a telegraph addressed to his father after the games, Frank wrote, "Dear Dad, thanks for waiting around for me to be born in 1924. I'm coming home with the gold medal you should have won. I did it for you Dad! Your loving son, Frank."

I love how this father sacrificed his own passion to be in the presence of his newly-born son. Years later, he coached his son to achieve the Olympic gold medal that he wanted. We all have dreams, and our dreams should be bigger than what can be accomplished in a lifetime. But what we cannot achieve, our children can pick up and finish. That's a great legacy!

The gold standard of parenting is to train our children to climb higher and go farther than what we ever dreamed. What are we passing on to our kids? What dreams of ours will they passionately pick up, carry on, and complete? Without a doubt, Kingdom purposes should be our highest family priority. But, we cannot simply assume past faithfulness will continue to our children and to their children. Each generation must be taught who God is, and what He has done for mankind.

The statistics present a real problem that affects our most prized possession: our kids and our grandkids. We need to pick up the same vision and passion that King David had developed in his older age. His words in Psalm 71:17–18 are poignant, "Since my youth, God, you have taught me, and to this day I declare your marvelous deeds. Even when I am old and gray, do not forsake me, my God, till I declare your power to the next generation, your mighty acts to all who are to come." David's cry was to fully empower his children and grandchildren.

The Bible clearly articulates that the age of a person is not important, but the faith we have in our God is important. Here are several examples from Scripture:

- 1 Timothy 4:12, "Don't let anyone look down on you because you are young, but set an example for the believers in speech, in conduct, in love, in faith and in purity."
- Numbers 11:28, "Joshua son of Nun…had been Moses' aide since youth…"
- 2 Chronicles 34:3, "…while [Josiah] was still young, he began to seek the God of his father David…"

The Bible talks much about the passing of a spiritual baton to the next generation. As leaders, we should always be on the lookout for the next relay runner. As we run our spiritual race, we always need to recruit three people on our relay team. We need a Paul, a Barnabas and a Timothy. Paul is the leader we can grow from. Barnabas is the one who will encourage us. Timothy is the one we can mentor. This combination of teammates will place you at the top of your game.

David Passes His Legacy to Solomon

David had a dream to build the house of God. Despite his dream, passion, intentions, and preparations, it remained an unfulfilled dream. 1 Chronicles 28:2 states, "King David rose to his feet and said: 'Listen to me, my fellow Israelites, my people. I had it in my heart to build a house as a place of rest for the ark of the covenant of the Lord, for the footstool of our God, and I made plans to build it.'" David had grown old in age and realized he was running out of time. So, David passed the baton to Solomon. David's dream became Solomon's destiny.

1 Chronicles 28:9–10 continues the account,

> And you, my son Solomon, acknowledge the God of your father, and serve Him with wholehearted devotion and with a willing mind, for the Lord searches every heart and understands every desire and every thought. If you seek Him, He will be found by you; but if you forsake Him, He will reject you forever. Consider now, for the Lord has chosen you to

build a temple as a sanctuary. Be strong and do
the work.

All David had without Solomon was a dream. All Solomon had without David was an unfulfilled destiny.

1 Chronicles 28:12, 19 states, "He gave him the plans of all that the Spirit had put in his mind for the courts of the temple of the Lord and all the surrounding rooms, for the treasuries of the temple of God and for the treasuries for the dedicated things. 'All this,' David said, 'I have in writing from the hand of the Lord upon me, and He gave me understanding in all the details of the plan.'"

When the younger generation, full of strength and energy, joins forces with an older generation, full of experience and wisdom, the results can be powerful and long-term. Every generation stands on the shoulders of those that went on before them.

This is a very clear vision with our family. My mom and dad, and Kay's mom and dad, set such an amazing spiritual foundation for us to build upon. Because of that great spiritual legacy, we've been able to soar past their greatest dreams and imaginations. We've ministered for the past forty years, and Kay and I are now watching our sons and their wives rising and succeeding beyond our greatest dreams and imaginations. Their responsibility is to set the standard for their sons and daughters to exceed their dreams in every possible way. Take pride in your family name and the calling of God upon your family.

My mom and dad grew up in Oklahoma. I remember my dad talking about harvest season, which was vital for their survival. All family members were needed to work in the fields. Sometimes school was even dismissed, and the field became the focus of everyone. It was not uncommon to see three generations working in the field together. Grandparents, parents, and children worked side-by-side because success and survival demanded it. In the same way, generations should learn how to run together, work together, and honor one another. Solomon took the baton from David and ran with it. David's lifelong dream to build the temple became Solomon's greatest accomplishment. The temple took seven years to build. It was built according to David's dream, David's design, and Solomon's wisdom. Simply put, the greatest gift each generation of leaders can leave is another qualified company of leaders.

Identifying the next generation of leaders isn't difficult, elusive, or vague. They are running around under your feet in your own home. Your legacy, and your children's success, greatly depends on how well you invest in them. I become weary hearing people talk about "Me Time." "Me Time" is not for warriors who want to change the world. I want "Investment Time." Investing is the only way to build equity. Investing in your children is your best investment! They are your apprentices, protégés, and successors. Their greatest gift in life is you. We increase our kids' swiftness and effectiveness at a young age by launching them from the platform we have built.

Common or Uncommon?

When my dad was twenty-seven-years old, he was dating my mom. They went to church one night and after hearing the message that night, he went to the altar and committed his life to Christ. My dad had no college degree. My mom worked her way through college getting a teaching degree with three young kids. They never made a lot of money. Neither of them ever spoke before crowds of people. Neither was publicly recognized for anything. Some would say they were as common as common could be. I wonder how many times they found themselves wondering what's the purpose of life, like most of us do at different times. We ask why we're here or what benefit we add to the world.

My parents raised three boys in the plains of West Texas, who grew up loving and respecting their parents, and learning to love the same things they loved. We fell in love with their God, and made their God our God. They gave life to two boys who became pastors and one who became a missionary. Within our three ministries, thousands have come to Christ. Countless numbers of those converts have gone into full-time ministry around the world, creating an exponential number of people coming to Christ on virtually every continent. To date, tens of thousands have been transformed by God's Word, because of a common young couple from the farmlands of Oklahoma lived out what they believed. Should they be labeled as common? Hardly! They are World Changers! That's the kind of legacy that's in front of us. We can produce kids who will enter every walk of life and impact people in their sphere of influence for Christ. Everyone has a story. What will the story sound like when your children tell it? Make it one worth telling over and over!

> *Not all spiritual champions have a spiritual heritage, but all spiritual champions leave a spiritual legacy to the next generation.*

CHAPTER 13

Praying for Our Kids

The great tragedy of life is not unanswered prayer, but unoffered prayer. Instead of prayer being something we do every day, like breathing, eating, walking and talking, it seems to have become like that little glass covered box on the wall that says, "Break in Case of Emergency." It is true that so very often we associate prayer with crises in our life. But, it's so much more than that.

Prayer is the enjoyment of a two-way communication with our creator. I believe that if you are in a relationship with somebody, you are going to have a high level of communication for the relationship to be healthy and strong. The same is true if you are in a relationship with God.

Your desire should be to talk to Him often, and to listen to what He has to say. It's very important for a Christian to develop a strong prayer life.

In 1 Thessalonians 5:16–18, Paul states, "Rejoice always, *pray continually*...for this is God's will for you in Christ Jesus." In Ephesians 6:18, he says, "And *pray in the Spirit on all occasions with all kinds of prayers and requests."* (Emphasis mine).

Prayer is imperative if we want God to be active in our life, our marriage, our home life and work life. In the first part of this book, I mentioned going to the church every morning to pray for our unborn children. That corner where I prayed, hovering over that vent, became my sacred place. For the next twenty-eight years, that was the place I met with God almost daily. It was the place I worshiped, rejoiced, and enjoyed my time with Him, but it also was the place I agonized through difficulties, betrayal, fear, disappointments, and depression. I shed a bucket of tears hovering over that vent all those years. But, it's remarkable to reflect over those twenty-eight years and remember all the miracles I watched God perform. The faithfulness of my God is astonishing. He is exactly who He says He is! I wouldn't trade that experience for anything in the world.

On our last Sunday in that building, before moving into our new facility, I was reminiscing that Sunday morning with our church congregation and being sentimental about all the wonderful things that had happened. As I talked about this one spot in the corner of the auditorium, I said, "Before I leave today, I'm going to pull that vent out of the floor and take it with me!" The next week was extremely busy as we were moving from our existing building to our new facility, and preparing for our Grand Opening. At the end of the week we turned the keys over to the new owners of our old building and later that day I remember thinking, "I forgot to get the vent." I wanted it as a reminder and a keepsake, and I was sad and frustrated I didn't get it.

The next Sunday was our Grand Opening, and everyone was beyond excited. You could feel the buzz in the air as everyone was working hard to make sure all ran smoothly. I can remember how nervous I was, pacing back and forth in a side room, knowing that this was the biggest day in the history of our church. About twenty minutes before service time, the back door opened and a couple walked in. They were on our leadership team and they said, "Pastor, we have a gift for you and we would like for you to open it before the service starts." As I tore open the wrapping paper, to my shock, I realized it was the floor vent they had mounted in a wooden frame! They said, "Pastor, we were part of the clean-up crew before handing over the keys in the old building. Before we left, we pulled the vent out of the floor because we knew how much it meant to you." Today that vent hangs on my office wall.

It is a spiritual marker that reminds me of the miracles that took place in my boys' lives because of prayer. Just as God told Israel to set stones in places to remind them of His protection and miracles, we need spiritual markers to remind ourselves of the power of prayer for our kids, and how we need to keep praying for them every day!

> *Prayer is talked about more than anything else, and practiced less than anything else. Yet for the believer, it remains one of the greatest gifts our Lord has given to us.*

You cannot be an overcoming Christian and not pray, in the same way you cannot have a good marriage if you don't talk to your spouse. Communication is always the pathway to relational intimacy. In the same way, prayer is the pipeline of communication and interaction between God and His people.

Prayer Changes Our Perspective

The reason prayer is an absolute necessity is because it changes our perspective. Prayer opens our spiritual eyes, enabling us to connect with God on a supernatural level.

In 2 Kings 6, Israel was surrounded by enemy armies, and Elisha's servant was afraid of being overtaken and destroyed. 2 Kings 6:15–17 reads,

> When the servant of the man of God got up and went out early the next morning, an army with horses and chariots had surrounded the city. "Oh no, my lord! What shall we do?" the servant asked. "Don't be afraid," the prophet answered. "Those who are with us are more than those who are with them." And Elisha prayed, "Open his eyes, Lord, so that he may see." Then the Lord opened the servant's eyes, and he looked and saw the hills full of horses and chariots of fire all around Elisha.

Divine communication gives insight. When we speak to God, God answers us and shows us things we do not know. In every difficult situation, we will tend to lean toward one of two perspectives: a human perspective or a spiritual perspective. Are we frightened by what we see, or strengthened by who's in control of our lives? What's our perspective? Do we believe God wants to give us His best?

Two of the most instructive parables where Jesus talked about relentless, persistent prayer are found in Luke 11 and Luke 18. The disciples had asked Jesus to teach them to pray. He told them two stories so they could better understand the nature of prayer and the Heavenly Father they are addressing.

Luke 11:5–9 reads,

> The Jesus said to them, "Suppose you have a friend, and you go to him at midnight and say to him, 'Friend, lend me three loaves of bread; a friend of mine on a journey has come to me, and I have no food to offer him.' And suppose the one inside answers, 'Don't bother me. The door is already locked, and my children and I are in bed. I can't get up and give you anything.' I tell you, even though he will not get up and give you the bread because of friendship, yet because of your shameless audacity he will surely get up and give you as much as you need. So I say to you, 'Ask and it will be given to you; seek and you will find; knock and the door will be opened for you.'"

In this story, we find a man who receives what he asks for because of his passionate persistence. He gets his request, not because his friend loves him, but because of his persistence in asking.

The passage in Luke 18 is the same teaching, told with different characters. Luke 18:1–5, "Then Jesus told his disciples a parable to show them that they should always pray and not give up. He said: 'In a certain town there was a judge who neither feared God nor cared what people thought. And there was a widow in that town who kept coming to him with the plea, "Grant me justice against my adversary." For some time he refused.'" Jesus goes on to say that the judge finally gave in, not because he believed in the widow's cause, but because he was weary of her bugging him.

In both cases, Jesus compares this, unbelievably, to praying to God. Seriously? Is Jesus comparing God to a non-caring friend or a grumpy old judge? Is He comparing God to someone who will eventually respond to you, not out of love, but because you are irritating him by your persistence. He finally gives in and gives you your request, because He doesn't want to be bothered by you any longer.

Jesus used parables often, and His parables always had a twist to them. It made the listener stop and think for a moment. His stories often had a certain level of shock value, causing people to shake their head in confusion and forcing them to think deeper. When we hear one of Jesus' parables, we usually relate to someone in the parable, and realize that someone in the parable is God. "So, which character is me? I must be the friend in need and God is the one inside telling me to go away. Or, I'm the needy widow, and God is the judge."

Everyone listening to the story is in shock. Then there is a short pause in the story. And slowly we begin to understand. Jesus' point is not to equate God to an irritated friend or an unjust judge, but He is showing God in contrast to them. We can understand that even if an unwilling friend or a mean judge would grant our request because of persistent asking, God, who loves us and cares for us, will give us exactly what we need.

Jesus concludes the parable with this statement in Luke 11:9. "So I say to you, 'Ask and it will be given to you; seek and you will find; knock and the door will be opened for you.'" Ask, seek and knock are verbs. They are action words in the present tense. They could be translated as, "keep on asking, keep on seeking, and keep on knocking." Don't give up too easily!

George Muller, known as one of the greatest prayer warriors of all time, wrote this about prayer in his *Narrative* in 1855, "It is a common temptation of Satan to make us give up too soon. The truth is, to enjoy the Word, we ought to continue to read it, and the way to obtain a spirit of prayer is to continue praying. The less we read the Word of God, the less we desire to read it, and the less we pray, the less we desire to pray."

We all need to be reminded how much God wants to interact with us and wants to meet our requests. Prayer is the greatest spiritual tool we have been given to build our spiritual lives.

Building Requires the Right Measurement

Building spiritually requires a certain kind of measurement. In the book of Genesis, the measurement Noah used while building the ark was called a cubit. A cubit is an ancient unit of length, which means an arm's length. The unit was based on the forearm length from the tip of the middle finger to the bend of the elbow. It was a crude form of measuring. A cubit is also made up of approximately six hand-widths from the bend of the arm to the end of the fingers. Six hand-widths equal a cubit. Six is important to note because six is the number of man. God created man on the sixth day and on the seventh day God rested. Seven is the number of God, meaning completion. By design, we are incredible creatures. There seems to be no end to our amazing accomplishments. We calculate, measure, and then build empires, kingdoms, and corporations. We have the ability to amass millions and millions of dollars. Yet, Jesus said in John 15:5, "...apart from me you can do nothing."

Why would he say that? After all, He created us with such intellectual and physical abilities. The answer: Jesus is focusing on something entirely outside the physical realm. He is informing us that we can do nothing that has eternal benefits without Him. All of us are in the process of building something. Whether it's building a marriage, building a family, building a career, or building for retirement, we are building something. By nature, we are builders, but that doesn't mean that what we build will always be beautiful and productive.

On one occasion, Jesus tells a story about two men. One

built his house upon sand and the other upon a rock. One had a firm foundation and could weather the storms. The other built upon the shifting sand and was destroyed by a storm. Both builders used calculations and measurements, yet one endured while the other was destroyed. How often do we see people enjoy extreme success and great wealth, while their own home life is falling apart? We are incredibly brilliant and, at the same time, we are so weak. We can be a great success in one area of our life and a complete failure in another. With this in mind, the Bible speaks of two kinds of cubits we will use while building our future. A physical cubit or a spiritual cubit.

In the Old Testament, in the book of Ezekiel, God gives Ezekiel a dream to build Him a house where the children will be blessed. Ezekiel 43:13 states that the measurements must be a royal cubit. The royal cubit is the length of a regular cubit, plus a hand-width. This is different than the physical cubit used by Noah in Genesis. The royal cubit measures differently, because it shifts from human measurements to heavenly, or supernatural, measurements.

God emphasizes "The Law of The House" in Ezekiel twice. He wants us to understand what it is. The royal cubit mentioned here is a supernatural type of measurement. We are instructed that whatever we choose to do, we should do it with everything in our own power, *and* add one more hand-width. *This hand-width is the hand of God.* If we want God working in our home, we must use "The Law of the House." It must be the Law in my house and the Law in your house.

> *It is living every day with a measure of God in every activity of our life.*

This is the only way to build our household in the 21st Century: maintain a marriage of love and friendship, raise our children in a dark world, and have a godly home environment of warmth and peace. Do all you can do in your own strength, then add one more hand-width, the hand of God. Don't build your home, your relationship with your spouse, or raise your children with only the skill of your own hands, but add one more hand—the hand of God. He will add an element of peace, power, protection, and direction for each family member that you cannot provide.

Angels Are Ministering Agents

Stories of angels in the Bible have always fascinated me. I believe the greatest tragedy of our absence of prayer is that an army of ministering angels that are never dispatched from heaven on our kids' behalf.

Parents, pray that God will send warring angels to walk with your children every day. Your voice activates heaven, and puts the supernatural into action. Angels are mentioned almost three hundred times in the Bible, and we find three categories of angels: Worshiping, Witnessing, and Warring Angels.

Many times, I've been asked this question, "Is there such a thing as guardian angels?" The belief of guardian angels comes from two different passages of scripture: Matthew 18:10 and

Psalm 91:11. Matthew 18:10 states, "See that you do not despise one of these little ones. For I tell you that their angels in heaven always see the face of my Father in heaven." Psalm 91:11 reads, "For He will command his angels concerning you to guard you in all your ways."

In both passages, we can clearly see God sending angels to interact with humans, but it's not clear if everyone is assigned with their own personal guardian angel. We do know the Bible refers to them as agents of God, and they play an enormous role in all our lives. We are fighting a spiritual battle every day of our lives. The enemy's desire is to destroy our children's future. Paul reminds us of this in Ephesians 6:10–12, "Finally, be strong in the Lord and in His mighty power. Put on the full armor of God, so that you can take your stand against the devil's schemes. For our struggle is not against flesh and blood, but against the rulers, against the authorities, against the powers of this dark world and against the spiritual forces of evil in the heavenly realms." The Apostle Paul also instructs us to walk in the Spirit daily. To walk in the Spirit simply means to constantly be aware of God's presence in your life.

Let me share a story with you about the importance of being in the presence of God. It's the story found in the Old Testament when King David was attempting to move the Ark of the Covenant back to Jerusalem. On the journey, Uzzah touched the ark and fell dead. It surprised and scared everyone, as they realized the force and power of the ark.

David was angry, confused, and unsure that he wanted to bring it into Jerusalem. He needed time to think, so they made a quick decision to store the ark in the home of Obed-Edom, who had a home nearby. The ark was placed inside his home. The presence of God was actually dwelling in his house, and it remained there for three months!

2 Samuel 6:11 states, "The ark of the Lord remained in the house of Obed-Edom the Gittite for three months, and the Lord blessed him and his entire household." Wow! I wonder what the blessing looked like?

Let me give you the definition of a blessing: It's a spiritual force that causes success, protection and happiness beyond what is deserved. Those observing Obed-Edom's blessing must have seen some astonishing things to report it to the king. What do you think his neighbors saw? Let me speculate. Perhaps peace and joy came to the family that had not been there before. Perhaps they had thriving crops, increased wisdom, confidence, or restored health and success in everything they did. Clearly there was no doubt that blessing had fallen upon them. Some on-lookers would call it unusual luck. Obed-Edom knew it wasn't luck, but the favor of God. All of this was freely given to him, because he was in close proximity to his God. He became the benefactor of a spiritual force called "blessing." His experience identifies for us today that there are higher ways of living available to us by simply being as close to God as we can possibly be.

2 Samuel 6:12 continues, "Now King David was told, 'The Lord has blessed the household of Obed-Edom and everything he has, because of the ark of God.' So David went to bring up the ark of God from the house of Obed-Edom to the City

of David with rejoicing." David desired to have all the same blessings that had been poured out on Obed-Edom. When King David arrived to take the ark back to Jerusalem, he was careful to do it exactly how God had instructed them to transport it. Then something else happened. When they removed the ark from Obed-Edom's home, he had no desire to live without being in the presence of God. He experienced it for three months, and realized he couldn't live without it. His desire for the Lord caused him to do whatever it took to stay close to the Lord. So, he followed King David as they paraded the ark back to Jerusalem to its new home.

Later in scripture we find Obed-Edom becomes the gatekeeper to the chamber where the ark was placed and the presence of God dwelled. The gatekeeper guards and protects the doorway as well as holding open the door for others to enter. Where did that door lead? To the ark and the presence of God! It led to the inner courts where people came face to face with their Holy God.

Parents, we are called, having tasted and seen that the Lord is good, to guide our children in the same direction we have gone. A doorkeeper is one who has been inside, face-to-face with God. When we have experienced the presence of God, nothing else matters to us but getting our children to the same door. Our number one objective is to personally introduce our children to this amazing God whose name is Jesus. We can never leave our post as a gatekeeper, but must stand constantly at the door of His presence, holding the door wide open for our children to enter.

Obed-Edom later becomes a worship leader and is mentioned along with Asaph, who was the Chief Musician. He and his sixty-eight associates led the nation in worship to their Lord. Yet, he continues to keep the gates. He is not only blessed in ministry, but also in his family relationships. God gave him eight sons. His sons, grandsons, and great-grandsons also worshiped the Lord and were blessed by the Lord. The Bible tells us that all of them were leaders, capable men, with strength to do the work of the ministry. That is remarkable! Not some of his descendants, or not even most of them were blessed. All sixty-eight were blessed! God blessed his whole household. This is what it means to leave a legacy!

Obed-Edom's faith and love for God was contagious to every family member. He created a family legacy of generational blessings. What a great example for us to follow. Prayer is the very thing that connects us to the presence of God. As we pray, we are drawing ourselves and our children into His presence. When our children experience God and not just religious acts, they too will chase God the rest of their lives.

How to Pray for Your Child

Your prayers are the biggest weapon you must use to protect and raise up godly children. Pray often for your children whenever they come to mind. Pray for them as you fold their socks, when you send them off to school, late at night as you tuck them into bed, or anytime you think of them throughout the day.

Even when I spend time in God's Word, if a scripture jumps off the page, I use it to pray over my kids at that very moment. Engaging the Bible and praying are the primary methods for developing a deepening relationship with God. While many tend to think of prayer and Bible reading as separate spiritual practices, they can be even more powerful when combined into one practice of "praying scripture."

Are you ever unsure about what you should pray? Do your prayers become dull or repetitive? Do you feel like you're praying "wrong?" Learn to pray the scriptures, and use the words and emotions of the Bible to gain more confidence in your prayers. From Genesis to Revelation, there are biblical prayers we can pray to strengthen our spiritual lives. These prayers express every kind of emotion and experience. The whole book of Psalms is a prayer book! By praying the prayers of the Bible, we identify with the biblical authors. The prayers of the Bible become our tutors to learn how to communicate with God.

Praying Scripture

Let me give you examples of praying scripture over our children.

Read the Scripture

Ephesians 6:13–17,

> Therefore put on the full armor of God, so that when the day of evil comes, you may be able to stand your ground, and after you have done everything, to stand. Stand firm then, with the belt of truth buckled around your waist, with the breastplate of righteousness in place, and with your feet fitted with the readiness that comes from the gospel of peace. In addition to all this, take up the shield of faith, with which you can extinguish all the flaming arrows of the evil one. Take the helmet of salvation and the sword of the Spirit, which is the word of God.

Pray the Scripture

This is how I would pray this passage over my children. "Father God, I invite you into my home and ask the Holy Spirit to rest on my children. As I send them out into the world today, I pray they walk in peace, instead of anxiety, stress, and insecurity. I pray that the belt of truth will be firmly worn, and that they will know the truth. Don't let the lies of the enemy affect them. I pray they will wear the breastplate of righteousness today, and by your guidance, they will make right decisions. I pray they will do what is right in your eyes. Lead them in all their choices.

I pray they will pick up the shield of faith. Father, I pray their faith will act as a shield to ward off the enemy's flaming arrows, and that they may have faith in the unseen, which is you. I pray as they walk out the door today, they will put on the helmet of salvation and pick up the sword, which is the Word of God. By their personal experience with you and their knowledge of your word, I pray You will protect their heart and mind. Lord, I pray for a hedge of protection around my children as they engage in the world today. Let your presence guide them, and your warrior angels fight for them. In Jesus' name, I pray, amen."

Read the Scripture

Joshua 1:9, "Have I not commanded you? Be strong and courageous. Do not be afraid; do not be discouraged, for the Lord your God will be with you wherever you go."

Isaiah 41:10, "So do not fear, for I am with you; do not be dismayed, for I am your God."

Pray the Scripture

"Lord Jesus, I pray that my children are strong and courageous when trouble comes. Please help them to not be frightened or distressed, but remind them of your promise that you are always with them wherever they go. Today, I declare my child will be strong and courageous to face any temptations or trouble that comes their way. I pray they will be highly aware of your constant protective presence that hovers over them all day long. In Jesus' name, I pray, amen."

Read the Scripture

Philippians 4:6–7, "Do not be anxious about anything, but in every situation, by prayer and petition, with thanksgiving, present your requests to God. And the peace of God, which transcends all understanding, will guard your hearts and your minds in Christ Jesus."

Pray the Scripture

"Lord Jesus, I pray that my children will not be anxious about anything, but instead they will let their requests be known to you. Please, Lord, give them the peace that surpasses all understanding. Bring them peace not only in times of great trial, but in all their daily routines. Lord, wrap your arms around them and guard their hearts and minds. In Jesus' name, I pray, amen."

Read the Scripture

James 1:5–6, "If any of you lacks wisdom, you should ask God, who gives generously to all without finding fault, and it will be given to you. But when you ask, you must believe and not doubt, because the one who doubts is like a wave of the sea, blown and tossed by the wind."

Pray the Scripture

"Lord Jesus, I pray that my children will know your wisdom, which will rid them of doubting. I pray that they seek your wisdom daily for all the decisions they will make. Please give them wisdom generously like you have promised, and help them to know it is from you. Please teach them not to be swayed by the opinions and beliefs of others, but to stay firm on what Your Word says. In Jesus' name, I pray, amen."

Read the Scripture

Psalm 139:23–24, "Search me, God, and know my heart; test me and know my anxious thoughts. See if there is any offensive way in me, and lead me in the way everlasting."

Pray the Scripture

"God, today as a parent leader, I ask you to search my heart. Challenge and reveal my wrongs, weaknesses, lusts, greed, hate, envy, or rebelliousness. Change my heart that's full of worry to a spirit of peace. Change my irritability to a spirit of patience. Change my negative spirit to a positive spirit. Lord, help me not to be deceived by allowing any thoughts to lead me astray. In Jesus' name, I pray, amen."

These are many examples of praying biblically. On one occasion, Jesus taught on prayer and gave us an outline on how to pray, known to us today as The Lord's Prayer. In Matthew 6:7, Jesus starts with this statement, "And when you pray, do not keep babbling on like the pagans, for they think they will be heard because of their many words." Notice He doesn't want us to fall into repetitious, redundant prayers, continually reciting something over and over. In no way is that any kind of meaningful conversation. God wants to hear your heartfelt words of passion and emotion. What is interesting, is the Lord's Prayer has been memorized and recited as if it were some kind of magic mantra that will bless people or move God in their direction. People are doing exactly what Jesus was instructing us not to do. The Lord's Prayer is an outline of how to pray, not simply words that should be recited without any meaning or power.

Jeremiah 29:12 reads, "Then you will call on Me and come and pray to Me, and I will listen to you." Prayer is a two-way conversation. I think there is a huge misconception that when we pray, we must pray long eloquent prayers for hours at a time, but that's not the case.

Throughout the day, God longs to hear our simple prayers:

- Thank you for this breakfast, Lord.
- Help me stay calm in this traffic jam.
- Lord, help me love this person right now.
- God, will you show me what to do?
- Dear God, give me wisdom right now.
- God, help me to love and serve my spouse.
- Lord, I love you.
- Goodnight, Lord.

Don't wait for the perfect time to sit down and pray. Don't wait until you have the perfect words. Don't wait because you feel dirty or sinful. Lift your voice to God in the morning, on the way to work, while you walk the dog, while making dinner, when feeling righteous or unrighteous. He stands ready to hear from you! Look to have prayer moments throughout the day and soon you will become a prayer warrior and a parent who is changing your children's lives, as well as generations to come.

BONUS SECTION

A View behind the Door of a Pastor's Home

Have you ever wondered what it's like behind the closed doors of the pastor's house? Do you ask yourself if the pastor lives the life that is preached about on Sunday? Or, is the preaching merely something that is spoken, and the real life is significantly different? This is your opportunity to not only peek behind the door, but to walk in and survey the entire space. Sit on the couch, or pull up a chair, and find out what it's like in a pastor's house.

CHAPTER 14

Pastor's Kids

After graduating from Bible college and preparing to go into full time ministry, I was filled with excitement. Kay and I got married and took our first ministry position. A couple of years later we started talking about having children. That discussion caused me great anxiety and fear. It was the realization that we were going to bring into this world a group of people called pastor's kids, or PK's. That was a terrifying thought, because I grew up in a generation where pastor's kids were the worst in the community.

At a friend's church, the pastor had a child who fell into this category. I watched as rebellion was unleashed not only in the pastor's home, but in the church. This pastor's kid despised God and everything the church stood for, bringing shame upon the family. Everybody in the church was horrified by the constant, embarrassing, sinful actions of this pastor's kid. The pain and scrutiny this pastor's family went through was excruciating. As a teenager, I had a front row seat of how a minister's home life can absolutely come unraveled.

The fear of this happening in my home was scary, but it was also a motivation that I would not let ministry have a negative effect upon my children. This sent me on a quest to know why so many times things go wrong in a minister's home, and what it takes to raise children who love the ministry and want to be a part of changing the world.

I searched the scriptures and found that it mentions a few PK's, or in this case, prophet's kids. Many of these followed a similar pattern of rebellion. Few of them loved the Lord and succeeded their fathers in the ministry. The big question is, "Why?"

When Samuel was growing up in the tabernacle, the sons of the High Priest, Eli, were breaking their father's heart. 1 Samuel 2:12 explains, "Eli's sons were scoundrels; they had no regard for the Lord." As I read this story in its entirety, these PK's took sin to new levels. "This sin of the young men was very great in the Lord's sight, for they were treating the Lord's offering with contempt" (1 Samuel 2:17). Eli's sons ultimately met an untimely death and brought great sorrow to Israel for generations.

I also read the tragic story of King David's family. These PK's, particularly Amnon and Absalom, were not exactly role models. In fact, David's sons ravaged the kingdom with sins such as rape, murder, rebellion, and treason. These sons caused David and the kingdom great pain and embarrassment.

I found that this story haunted me, causing me to ask myself, "How can a godly leader like King David raise such rebellious children?" Raising children in this fallen world to grow up and love the Lord and His church, and be faithful followers of Christ will not happen easily or naturally. Raising kids in a pastor's home adds another level of difficulties and challenges.

Pastoral Statistics

As stated by the Barna Group, the statistics of those who choose to go into full-time ministry are bleak and disturbing, but they reveal the battle we are facing. The percentages are shown of those who answered a particular question affirmatively:

- Pastors who report working between fifty-five and seventy-five hours per week (90 percent).
- Pastors who feel unable to meet the demands of the job (50 percent).
- Pastors who are grossly underpaid (70 percent).
- Pastors who feel they are inadequately trained to cope with ministry demands (90 percent).
- Pastors who said the ministry was completely different than they thought it would be (90 percent).
- Pastors who constantly fight depression (70 percent).
- Pastors who feel so discouraged that they wished they could leave the ministry, but have no other way of making a living (50 percent).
- Seventeen hundred pastors leave the ministry each month.
- Ministers starting out will not be in full-time ministry five years later (50 percent).

- Only one out of every ten ministers will retire as a minister.
- Four thousand new churches begin each year, but seven thousand churches close.

Pastor's families are negatively impacted as well:

- Pastors who believe pastoral ministry has negatively affected their families (80 percent).
- Spouses who feel their pastor spouse is overworked, or feel left out and under-appreciated by church members (80 percent)
- Spouses who do not have someone they consider a close friend (70 percent).
- Spouses who report serious conflict with a parishioner at least once a month (40 percent).

Whether someone is a full-time pastor or a bi-vocational minister, balancing both a job and a church can create personal and family stress. This can lead to discouragement and depression. It's understandable why so many PK's are so turned off by this church thing.

PK's: Expected to Perform on Command

I heard about a young adult whose experience growing up as a Pastor's Kid caused him to struggle with depression and even attempt suicide on multiple occasions. Growing up, he consistently experienced church taking priority over every aspect of his life: school events, family vacations, and even just a day spent together with the family. He said that his parents expected him to perform on command, and that there was an inevitable spotlight which shined on him during his formative years. "Just being a kid" was not an option for him. To his parents, he was an extension of their ministry, and was expected to perform perfectly at every church-related function. To this day, he still resents the life he felt forced into, and wrestles with even being a part of the church in his adult life.

A recent article by Dale Hudson in Ministry Today Magazine describes Katy Perry as the highest profile PK that has walked away from the faith. It goes on to say, "She is no longer a Christian and doesn't believe in heaven, hell or an 'old man sitting on a throne.'"

More sobering statistics from Barna Group research state:

- PK's who have gone through a period where they significantly questioned their faith (40 percent).
- PK's who are no longer active in church (33 percent).
- PK's who no longer consider themselves a Christian (7 percent).

When asked what was difficult about their childhood and teen years, PK's responses were sobering:

- PK's who felt unrealistic expectations were placed on them (28 percent).
- PK's who felt they had negative experiences in church (18 percent).

- PK's who felt their father or mother were too busy at church to spend time with them (17 percent).
- PK's who felt that the Christian faith was not modeled at home (14 percent).
- PK's who were influenced by friends or peers (9 percent).

Pastors were asked what they would change:

- "Spend more time with their kids" (42 percent).
- "Be more understanding of their kids" (8 percent).
- "Give my child more spiritual guidance" (5 percent).
- "I wouldn't change anything and have no regrets" (19 percent).

PK'S: Betrayed by Church People

Another PK story I heard is that of a young woman who experienced incredible hypocrisy from people within her parent's congregation. In her young life, she watched as her parents were betrayed, turned on, and lied to in almost every church community they served. Over the course of her childhood, her parents lost their jobs at multiple churches in different cities, and the family was forced to regularly pick their lives up and move to a new community. Because of these experiences, this PK had a massive sense of anxiety around creating authentic relationships, and built up walls to keep anyone from coming close to her. While her parents saw ministry gifts within her and encouraged her to pursue full-time ministry, she was so scared and turned-off by her experience in the church that she ran in the complete opposite direction. The lack of trust, lack of real relationships, and lack of stability in her early life caused her to resent her upbringing and walk away from the church completely.

These kinds of feelings from PK's are what concerned me. I wanted my kids to believe that ministry is the greatest privilege in the world and that their "pastor dad" enjoyed life at its highest levels. In addition, I made the mental decision from the very beginning that however difficult ministry became, I would not bring home negativity to impact our family life. That sounds easier than it is.

Three years into pastoring we experienced one of the worst church splits imaginable. The tension brewed and mounted for more than a year surrounding my desire to change our church's vision and direction from what the church had held sacred for over fifty years. In one week, half of the church walked out to start their own church two miles down the road. It's hard for me to even describe the pain we experienced. People that we had given our life, service and ministry to walked out angry, saying incredibly hurtful things. It felt like an insurmountable situation as we tried to survive and keep the church doors open.

We walked through that devastation for the next several years. With a broken spirit, I wept every day for over a year. However, I personally vowed that when I went home, I would not cast a negative light upon the church with my family. And, I never did. At all times, we must keep our bearings and never lose sight that the church is our calling and the hope of the world.

2 Timothy 2:1–7 declares,

> You then, my son, be strong in the grace that is in Christ Jesus. And the things that you have heard me say in the presence of many witnesses entrust to reliable people who will also be qualified to teach others. Join with me in suffering, like a good soldier of Christ Jesus. No one serving as a soldier gets entangled in civilian affairs, but rather tries to please his commanding officer. Similarly, anyone who competes as an athlete does not receive the victor's crown except by competing according to the rules. The hardworking farmer should be the first to receive a share of the crops. Reflect on what I am saying, for the Lord will give you insight into all this.

We accepted the call to stand on behalf of Christ in our church, not only believing in Him, but also suffering for His sake. The Christian leader is called to endure hardships. Paul gives us a laundry list of his trials in 2 Corinthians 11:22–33. Ministry difficulties and hardships should not catch us off guard because we have willingly volunteered. We are a soldier in battle, a farmer during harvest, an athlete in the Olympics, and committed to God's purpose. If we serve in the military, we don't run from battle, but run to it. We continue to fight until we overcome. We who are in the ministry must see ourselves as active-duty military during time of war.

Consider the "Eleven General Orders" that guide the U.S. Navy. Every military branch has a similar set of orders. Read a few of these orders:

- To walk my post in a military manner, keeping always on the alert, and observing everything that takes place within sight or hearing.
- To report all violations of orders I am instructed to enforce.
- To quit my post only when properly relieved.
- To be especially watchful at night, and during the time for challenging, to challenge all persons on or near my post and to allow no one to pass without proper authority.

Compare those to the "Eleven General Orders" found in Ephesians 6:10–20 that should guide every Christian leader:

- Be strong with the Lord's mighty power.
- Put on all of God's armor so that you will be able to stand firm against all strategies and tricks of the devil.
- Use every piece of God's armor to resist the enemy in the time of evil, so that after the battle is over, you will still be standing firm.
- Stand your ground, hold on to the truth and the body armor of God's holiness.

- Bind yourself to the Spirit of the Lord and the gospel of peace.
- In every battle, you will need faith as your shield to stop the fiery arrows shot at you.
- Cover your head with the helmet of salvation, and take the sword of the Spirit with you into battle, which is the word of God.
- Pray at all times and on every occasion in the power of the Holy Spirit.
- Stay alert and be persistent in your prayers for all Christians everywhere.
- Ask God to give you the right words to explain his message of salvation.
- Love with faith, as an ambassador of the Lord Jesus Christ filled with the power of the Holy Spirit.

It's imperative that we never forget what we have signed up to do. It's war. No matter how messy or difficult ministry becomes, our family knows we don't leave anyone behind. Our spouses and children must never forget our great calling.

Glass House Syndrome

PK's feel that they grow up with the members of the church viewing them this way. The insecurities of the pastor/parent needing to impress others by their family life, or protecting the "office of the pastor" can bring a dangerous pressure upon our kids. People will unintentionally expect more from them. They will hear phrases throughout their entire childhood from church attendees and church staff members such as:

- I expect more of you because you're the pastor's kid.
- You can't talk like that, you're the pastor's kid.
- A pastor's kid should know better than to run in church.

Well-meaning members of the church who say these things have no understanding how destructive these statements can be. Couple that with the comments made at school by teachers, coaches, and peers when they find out a child is a pastor's kid. PK's can believe their life is strangely different, or somehow abnormal, and the pastor's house is the home that none of their friends want to go to. The pastor's house seems like a strict, rigid environment and certainly would not be the place to spend time. The unspoken, uncomfortable thought is, "Can you imagine trying to have fun with a pastor sitting in the house with us?"

We found that way of thinking to be true with our kids' friends from school. When our boys were in high school, it was a struggle to get their friends to come to our house. We kept telling our kids to invite their friends over, but there seemed to be resistance.

Once the ice was broken, however, Kay and I worked hard on making it a fun place to be, providing food, drinks and desserts. We watched movies late into the night. Those nights were filled with so much fun and laughter. Over time, their friends didn't want to go anywhere else. Over the next few years, our house was packed with their friends from school every weekend. We built a great relationship with all their friends, and we cherish those days as some of our fondest memories.

Our family worked hard on turning the negative term, "glass house," into a positive term. We wanted their friends to look at our home life, family life, personal life and see what a real relationship with Jesus looks like. When it's authentic, it's the most fun anyone will ever experience. We invited them to come and join the party, and they did!

PK's Have a Unique Life

As a pastor/parent, you set the tone, attitude, and atmosphere of what it means to be a PK. I'm not sure our kids ever viewed themselves as PK's. They saw themselves as a kid whose dad just happens to be a pastor. Our three boys are now grown, married and have their own children, and all of them look back and say, "I loved my life growing up in the ministry." Here are three great ways to help your kids view their unique life as a special life:

Being a PK is an Honor and a Blessing

Being a PK gives privileges and opportunities most children never have. PK's will go to conferences, on mission trips and youth trips (even if they're not old enough to go). PK's will meet some of the greatest leaders in the country, and spend time with them at dinners after services.

The church can become one of the greatest playgrounds in

the world. PK's can swim in the baptistery, slide down the stair banisters, play hide and seek under the auditorium chairs, and play the drums on stage as loud as they want. The church is the place where best friends are made. What an amazing place!

Often the most talented singers, speakers, and most confident leaders in the world are PK's who have been brought up in church. PK's are enormously blessed to be surrounded by great leadership. Growing up in ministry, many times we step into leadership roles because there is no one else. By doing so we grow in ability and confidence, and are set far above our peers in leadership, greatly advancing our future opportunities.

> *It's an uncommon opportunity that we should value and not overlook.*

Expect Some to be Unkind

We should lower our expectations of people in the church. First, we won't be so disappointed when someone is harsh and unkind. Second, we will appreciate more those who are loving, generous, and kind. Don't expect everyone in church to be Christ-like and understanding. This is a setup for disappointment.

Always remember that anyone can join a church, no matter their mental health or maturity level. Churches attract all kinds of people: Godly people, sinful people, sweet people, mean people, atheists, agnostics, hypocrites, religious people, spiritual people, sincere people, humble people, loving people.

The thought that everybody in church should act like Jesus is a misconception. There are numerous people in the church that act like the devil. But, that's why we want these people coming to our churches. We are in the transformation business. It can be dangerous work at times because sheep bite, and people are not perfect. The church is made up of people who struggle and have weaknesses like we all do. Be mentally prepared and don't let the harshness of a few people hurt you or turn you sour toward the church. As Jesus hung on the cross in Luke 23:34, he looked toward heaven and prayed for those who were crucifying him, "Father, forgive them, for they do not know what they are doing." What a great example for us as leaders to follow.

Instead of becoming offended, bitter, and disillusioned with ministry, we remember our mission and pray for those who wrong us. We open our doors to messed up, hurting people. That's why we do what we do. And, it's why Jesus did what He did. We are here to love even unlovable people. We are in the people business, investing in the good, bad, and the ugly.

PK's are in the Public Spotlight

Many people, such as a celebrity or extremely-accomplished athlete, find themselves in the world spotlight. This level of recognition is what most people wish for, but the ones who have obtained it most often resent it. Living in a glass house where every eye is on them makes them feel like there is no room for mistakes. People watch. People tell them how to act. People have a standard for them. The public spotlight is a pressure and weight few kids can handle.

An online article published by Dr. Christina Villareal on March 26, 2010, explored the negative psychological impact of being highly visible in the public spotlight and the tremendous toll on one's psychological functioning:

> Everything celebrities do is publicized for the world to see, discuss, and mock. We love reading about the gaffes and gossip of the rich and famous, the more embarrassing, the better. A celebrity's natural response to this level of intense scrutiny is increased self-consciousness and paranoia. Many celebrities, particularly those in the political arena, grow weary of the unrealistic standards they are held to, and begin to feel resentful of the limitations of being in the public spotlight. They may "act out" in response to feeling suffocated by their carefully constructed public image. Self-destructive, acting out behaviors often include unsavory sexual appetites, scandalous liaisons, volatile outbursts, or other destructive patterns such as uncontrolled substance use. Exposure of their behaviors by the media can lead to overwhelming feelings of shame when their public image is destroyed.

By no means am I placing PK's into the celebrity category, but there are strong similarities due to the spotlight. PK's must navigate through the same psychological process of self-consciousness and paranoia. They may not have national recognition or the eye of the world, but they do experience the glaring spotlight in their own little world that can be as intense. People in the church know far more personal things about PK's than any other kid in the church. They know where PK's are going to college, who they took to prom, what kind of grades they made in school, or what kind of car they drive. They'll whisper, "Did you see he or she got a tattoo?" However, there is tremendous good attached to this as well. Teach your kids that their notoriety has been given to them as a gift. In every situation in life, they should find the good. Being a PK is a gift granted by God.

2 Chronicles 16:9 states, "For the eyes of the Lord range throughout the earth to strengthen those whose hearts are fully committed to Him." God is watching too, but not with an evil intent. He's looking around to see whom He can bless. Likewise, there are so many church members who love and care for PK's, or keep a protective eye on them. Many take them under their wing and made a positive difference in their life.

Over the course of raising our kids in church, there have been so many amazing people who stepped into our lives and loved our kids, nurtured them, spent time with them, and blessed them. I have recognized and identified them as gifts God sent into our lives. I am thankful for all the people that took time to invest into our children and would hate to think of raising them without these beautiful people. Every eye is on the PK, but there is a host of people encouraging you.

Pastors, pastors' wives, and PK's, don't get bitter, but thank God that He has divinely set you apart for the greatest work on the planet. You can help your PK's love their life by adding three simple but powerful ingredients: prayer, love and time.

Prayer

I've prayed for our children since before they were ever born. Throughout every stage of their lives, I've battled for them in prayer. This is by far the most important thing you will ever do as a parent. Throughout their teen years, there were many things that concerned me: their attitude changes, their friend choices, and the girls they decided to date.

When I felt my kids were being bombarded by the enemy to distract them from fulfilling their destiny in life, I always did the same thing. I would get in my car and drive on Interstate 25 to Santa Fe. I would make a loop and drive all the way back. I call it my Santa Fe prayer trail. I would be praying fervently and loudly all the way, forty-five minutes there and forty-five minutes back. Every time that I felt a tremendous war being waged against my kids, I took that trip, and I always saw the tremendous victories those prayers would bring. That round trip to Santa Fe has undoubtedly become my greatest asset as a parent. As ministers, we are notorious for thinking about praying and studying about praying. We will even ask people to pray for us. Too rarely do we break away and do spiritual warfare by praying for our children. When we are desperate, our prayer will move heaven and earth.

Children need to see and know that their parents are awestruck by the goodness and faithfulness of their God, and they will become awestruck as well.

Love

There are few things that I love more than the church. I have great affection toward it and the people who attend. It is vital for us to verbalize that love in front of our kids. As much as we love our church, we must never express that in a way that makes our children feel that we love it more than them. Church and children are not in competition with one another. As pastors, we are called to love and guide our children first. In fact, according to scripture, a man must be a good father before he's even qualified to be an elder or spiritual leader (1 Timothy 3:4–5). One of the ways we make a strong statement to our kids is to control our ministry schedule, instead of allowing the ministry or people to control our schedule.

For pastors, the intimidation factor plays a big part. We feel we must jump and run every time the phone rings. I battled this continually when we had a small congregation. Everyone had my phone number, and everyone seemed to have an urgent need. I ran to every call, because I wanted them to accept me, and be pleased that I was their pastor. If someone was being rushed to the hospital, going through surgery, or their marriage was falling apart, I ran to them, because I felt they needed me immediately. If a child was rebelling, I'd meet someone for coffee. If someone stubbed their toe, I'd be asked to stop what I was doing to pray for them. Yes, it got that ridiculous.

One afternoon, I took our boys to play golf. It was the first time I had played in over a year. We were on the second hole, when I received a call from a needy family. They called me constantly whenever a problem would arise, and they had lots of problems. I answered the phone standing on the green of the golf course, because I believed I needed to be available for the people I pastored. On the other end was a lady frantically crying, "They rushed my mother to the hospital. You have to go now. It's an emergency!" I told my kids we had to go because of an emergency. I will never forget their disappointment as we walked to the car. I took our kids home and quickly drove to the hospital. I walked into the hospital room, expecting to see someone on their death bed. Instead this lady was sitting in bed eating ice cream and watching television. That was the turning point for me. I knew that if I kept running blindly to people's needs and avoiding the needs of my own family, I was headed in the wrong direction.

I established new rules and guidelines that my family always came first. I learned to say to people, "I'm not coming now, but call me after the doctor assesses the situation." I learned to say, "I'm unable to meet you today, but I have time tomorrow." As the pastor, you must set boundaries, because if you don't, someone else will. Your kids must grow up knowing you love the church and you love people, but you love them more. Pastoring is like being self-employed. Here is a true saying, "The great thing about being self-employed is that you can work whenever you want. The bad thing about being self-employed is that you can work all the time."

Pastoring gave me a lot of flexibility to spend time with my kids, such as going on field trips, attending their sporting events and their practices every afternoon. I even coached some of their soccer, baseball, and football teams. If you asked my kids today, they'd say they love the work I'm in because it enabled us to do many things together. Being in a ministry family has special challenges, but also unique blessings. Using this flexible time wisely makes a big difference.

I had a friend in college who was a PK and, sadly, his experience growing up in a pastor's home was not a good one. He often talked about his family vacations in such a way that indicated to me there was a wedge between him and his dad. This should have been a fun and exciting time, but it was the very thing he resented from his childhood. He told me that every year he and his family would go to the mountains. He said they would rent a cabin, but his dad would go fishing every day and leave the family behind. His mom would tell the boys their dad needed time by himself. My friend elaborated on how much he hated vacations because his dad made it all about him and never about the family. He would always end those conversations with, "I hate vacations!"

That story impacted me greatly. I've never forgotten it. Every vacation we planned for our family, my friend's words stuck with me. When our kids were young and we would plan our vacations, I would have loved to have some "Me Time."

Peace and quiet are always desirable, but my friend's painful words would return to me, so I did everything in my power to make vacation about my family and not about me. Vacations over time became this crazy, intense competition between our three boys and me.

Kay enjoyed sitting back watching me trying to out-swim them and out-run them, or beat them at ping pong, racquetball, basketball. Everything was a competition. When I got back home, I needed a vacation from my vacation! However, we had a lot of fun, and we created memories for a lifetime. I wouldn't trade any of that for "Me Time."

Time

PK's discover quickly that a minister is never off the clock. People recognize us everywhere we go, whether the grocery store, a restaurant, or sporting event. There are seemingly non-stop phone conversations, emails, texts, and social media posts that can make kids feel they never have the full attention of their parents. One of the ways I combatted this was to give my kids permission to interrupt me. Why? Because my kids are always the most important people in the room.

I remember one Sunday morning, standing in the foyer of our church, there was a line of people waiting to talk to me. As I looked down the line, I saw our middle son, Jonathan, standing in the line patiently waiting to talk to me. The moment I saw him, I motioned for him to come to the front of the line. I said, "Jonathan, you never have to stand in line to talk to me. You can interrupt any conversation." I wanted our kids to know they are deeply cherished and valued, and they will never have to stand in line to talk to me.

Many times after church, I would spend a long time visiting with people, and I knew our kids would grow weary waiting on dad. I would catch their attention and call them over. As I continued the conversation, I would hug on my kids and draw them into the conversations. Many times, I would change the course of the conversation to include them or tell of something exciting that had happened to them that week. I intentionally wanted our kids to know that this church thing isn't something dad does, but what we do as a family.

Fixing Hearts and Breaking Hearts

Dr. Christiaan Barnard was born in 1922 in South Africa. As a cardiac surgeon living in Cape Town, he made history by performing the world's first heart transplant. This still remains the most publicized event in medical history.

In Dr. Barnard's book, *One Life*, he wrote about his enormous medical success and worldwide fame. While enjoying international notoriety, he revealed the biggest mistake he made and the extreme pain it brought into his life. Tragically, his story is far too common and continues to be repeated. He recounts in his book the most painful day of his life:

> I had spent months on in-depth research preparing my team of doctors and staff for the

first heart transplant to ever be attempted. After such a long time of being away, it was time to go home. I drove to New York and boarded a plane for South Africa. When I arrived my wife was there with our kids. I was unprepared for the greeting I received. "Why did you bother to come back home? Why didn't you stay in America?" There was no longer a light in her eyes nor a smile on her lips. "O God," I thought, I've made the worst mistake of my life. "Don't look so surprised," she said, "we've moved on, we realize we weren't important any longer to you." I quickly reminded her, "I wrote you two months ago and told you we were on the cusp of a historical medical breakthrough. We were building aortic valves for the transplant." In return she said, "You were also building a family, until you dumped it into my lap." I wanted to say something, but what. Anything I would say would sound meaningless and empty. I had become so busy and focused on fixing the hearts of the world, I broke the heart of my own family.

When I read his biography I found myself filled with a mixture of sadness and fear. I realized it is easy to chase after our dreams, accomplishments, recognition, and the applause of people, while our children feel forgotten and less important.

This kind of story continues to be repeated among church leaders and pastors. They are consumed at work and have nothing left to give their family when they get home. Sadly, this life pattern always results with the same outcome: relational destruction and heartbreak.

Pastors and church leaders, we need to burn the words of Dr. Barnard into our memory so they are never forgotten. Remember his words, "I had become so busy and focused on fixing the hearts of the world, I broke the heart of my own family."

We cannot be that kind of leader, bringing that kind of pain into our lives and our children.

Adjusting Your Schedule

When I took over as pastor, the schedule was grueling. It seemed like every night there was something happening that I wanted to attend. Dustin was playing high school football and the Junior Varsity games were on Wednesday nights, right in the middle of our midweek service.

I remember how disappointed he was when he handed me the game schedule, knowing that I was going to miss every game. At that time, our church was so small that I had no one to fill in and preach for me. I also knew there wasn't a chance I was going to allow this to be a sour memory, because his dad missed every game due to church. My creative juices started flowing. On Wednesday nights, I would back my car up to the back doors of the church. Instead of starting the service with the worship, I moved the teaching time to the front of the service. At 6:30 p.m., I started teaching and then finished with a prayer. I said, "Amen," and as the worship team was heading to the stage, I was heading out the back door.

I knew there would be complaints from some people because their schedule was disrupted, but I always reminded myself that in six months, the complainers will have forgotten the schedule change, but my son would remember me missing his games for the rest of his life. With that, my decision to change the schedule became a no-brainer.

Building fond memories is one the of the greatest gifts you will ever give your kids. When our kids were young, Kay had to work every Monday night. Instead of allowing that to be a negative, we turned it into a positive. Every Monday night for years we had "Men's Night Out." That is one of the biggest things our kids remember from their childhood.

We went to every pizza place, burger joint, and hole-in-the-wall restaurant imaginable. The only agenda was to have fun, and we did! I intentionally did my best on these Monday nights not to get on to them, talk about grades, or get frustrated if they made a mess at the table. Monday nights were designed to have fun, and we were going to do it with all our might. Now, twenty years later, I will drive by one of the pizza restaurants we used to go to, wishing my boys were still little. At the same time, I am so incredibly thankful for all the memories. Even in short moments with your kids, fully engage with them. Give them the best you have, even if it's only ten minutes, because you never know which moment will become the memory that they will cherish forever.

Letters from PK's: My Sons

In addition to my son, Dustin, who wrote the foreword to this book, I wanted to include two more letters from my sons, Jonathan and Brandon, and their first-hand accounts of being PK's.

Letter from Jonathan

I have a unique perspective of how it was growing up as a pastor's kid. I am not in full-time ministry. I currently serve on the Board at the Church, my wife and I are faithful attenders and we are involved in hosting small groups. However, for my full-time career, I am a pharmacist. I'd like to share what it was like growing up in a pastor's home while not being called into the ministry. It seems like it would be easy to have feelings of inferiority or disappointment from my parents, since my two brothers were both called into ministry. In fact, it was the exact opposite of that. From a young age, I have always had a special desire for learning and succeeding in school. My parents caught onto this very early, and from that point, they encouraged me to develop that gift.

They were always pushing me to take advanced classes and to make the honor roll. They were always there to support me when things got tough. My parents even played a pivotal role in getting me to be interested in pharmacy school. During my freshman year at college, my parents had met a woman at the church who had just graduated from pharmacy school. They knew that I was interested in something related to science or medicine, so they had me meet her and set up a tour of the college. About 6 years later, I graduated with a Doctor of Pharmacy degree and started working. Almost immediately after that, while I was working, I noticed my dad wandering through the aisles. He was so eager to see me as a pharmacist and wanted to watch me doing what I had been working so hard towards. As a pharmacist, I get to have one-on-one contact with hundreds of people a week, and during these times, I have the opportunity to love people and serve people to a level that we are commanded by God, as Christians. I get to build relationships and minister to people in a unique way.

My wife and I have kids of our own now, and what I experienced growing up is so valuable now that I am a parent. Instead of pushing my own desires on my kids, I will be actively observing and trying to pick up on the gifts God has given them. We are all called to ministry, and there are so many ways we can do that.

Letter from Brandon

I've always loved being a pastor's kid. I grew up SURROUNDED by people and in a constant flow of activity. The pace was fast, the days were full, and there never seemed to be a dull moment. For as long as I can remember, our family was at the church every time the doors were open. Sunday services, Wednesday night youth gatherings, Christmas and Easter rehearsals and productions, Harvest Festivals, all-church potlucks, weddings, funerals - the church was our second home, and its people were our extended family. We would hang out at the church for hours every day after school, so as a young kid I got into all kinds of trouble. I remember sneaking onto the roof because I had nothing better to do, and telling adults they couldn't tell me what to do because my dad was the pastor (this only happened once—my parents shut that down really quick)!

I learned early that it's important not to do life alone. My family would host get-togethers at the house, gathering people for conversation, laughter, and connection. I remember late-night grocery store runs to get food for a family that was in need...and I remember our own needs being met by the people within our church family. I look back on my unique upbringing with thousands of fond memories and, honestly, little to no regrets.

I want to be careful, however, not to paint it all as perfect. There were, indeed, moments that I didn't want to be at the church. There were situations when I could feel people's watchful eyes and I just wanted to be left alone. There were nights when I saw my parents exhausted and burdened because of the requirements and demands of ministry. There were also times when I could physically see the hurt my parents carried as the result of betrayal from people they trusted or poor, life-altering decisions made by people they loved dearly.

Ministry can be tough, and it can be especially tough on families. I've seen pastors that led thriving churches, and seemed to have it all together, but behind closed doors, their families were completely crumbling. I honestly believe that full-time ministry, if not handled carefully and intentionally by the parents, can be one of the most devastating things for families. I often hear about "crazy PK's" who are living double lives behind their parents' backs or collapsing from the pressure of having to project a "perfect" life, or losing faith in God altogether because of a disconnect between what dad preached and what dad actually lived out at home.

That's why I so appreciate the example set by my dad and so believe in the contents of this book. He has given absolutely all he could to the church, but somehow managed to give even more to his family. He's been consistent, faithful, loving, patient, encouraging, a servant, humble, wise, forgiving and, most importantly, he's always been there. He truly exemplified Paul's words in 1 Corinthians 11:1 when he wrote, "Follow my example, as I follow the example of Christ."

Now that I'm in full-time ministry, married and a new dad, I've become even more grateful for the example he set for me and my two brothers.

You can trust what's written in this book. He lived it!

A Healthy Family

The life of a pastor is not easy, and often, what is happening in the church can affect our families if we're not intentional in our parenting. Our boys were not isolated away from these painful times. They knew what we were experiencing when we went through a church split, or when people made false accusations about us. They lived their lives in the glass house that PK's experience. But we never allowed those hurts to change who we are as a healthy family.

There is nothing more important in life than this: your family will be healthy if you give it time. Family time is an essential factor that helps to create strong bonds, love, connections, and relationship among the family members. Spending quality time with family helps in coping with challenges, instills a feeling of security, inculcates family values, fills kids with confidence, and much more.

The King of Rock and Roll

Elvis Presley was an American singer and actor who is regarded as one of the most significant cultural icons of the 20th Century. He is often referred to as the "King of Rock and Roll," or simply, "The King."

Elvis achieved a level of celebrity status few have known: the fame, the wealth, the popularity, and stardom. He literally had everything the world had to offer. After many years of touring the world and packing out large venues full of cheering fans, he found himself lonely and empty on the inside.

In 1972 he recorded a song titled, "It's a Matter of Time." The song reveals his longing to go back to a place of warmth, fond memories, and the embrace of his own family. He had chased the glitz and glamour far too long, and was left with a hole in his heart. As Elvis sang about the life he had lived and the long time he had spent waiting, he simply wanted to go home.

We all have a longing to go back home. It doesn't matter whether you've had the best vacation ever or the worst week at work, there is only one place you want to go at the end of the day... Home!

People travel far and wide to see every corner of the globe, but they always wind up in the same place, because, let's face it, there's no place like home. For your kids, your time spent with them is like precious jewels that are embedded in their memories forever. The joy of family is truly "a matter of time."

Having somewhere to go is Home.

Having someone to love is Family.

Having both is a Blessing.

SPEAKING INQUIRIES FOR GALEN WOODWARD

If you would like to bring Galen Woodward to speak at your church, conference, or event, you can contact him at:

Citizen Church, Albuquerque, NM

505-299-7202

www.gwoodward.org

TOPICS INCLUDE:

Family Life

- Raising World Changers
- Prayer that Makes a Difference
- Parental Foundations
- Traits of a Generational Leader
- Building a Legacy
- Your Words Will Mold Your Children

Kingdom Builders Events

- Speaking to High-Capacity Leaders
- Launching Kingdom Builders in Your Church
- Investing in the Next Generation

Leadership

- Growing the Capacity of Your Church Staff
- Transforming Your Church to be Relevant in Your Community
- Leadership Talk: What I've Learned in 35 Years of Ministry